Mexican American Theatre:
Then and Now

Edited by Nicolás Kanellos

Arte Público Press
Revista Chicano-Riqueña
Houston, 1983

Mexican American Theatre: Then and Now was first published in 1983 as a special issue of *Revista Chicano-Riqueña*. The present reprint edition is made possible through support from the Ford Foundation.

Arte Público Press
University of Houston
Houston, Texas 77204-2090

ISBN 0-934770-22-0
LC. 83-070675

Dedicated to those artists who lived for the stage and helped to make this volume a reality.

Leonardo García Astol
Susie Mijares Astol
Belia Areu Camargo
Mateo Camargo
Rosalinda Fernández
La Familia García (Carpa García)
Eva Garza
Pedro "Ramirín" González y González
Lydia Mendoza
Beatriz "La Chata" Noloesca
Rafael Trujillo
Carolina Villalongín

CONTENTS

Introduction

Mexican American Theatre: Then and Now is a collection of materials created for and generated from an exhibit, "Two Centuries of Hispanic Theatre in the Southwest," that toured for one year to major museums in Arizona, California, New Mexico and Texas, with funding from the humanities councils of those states. Included here are the exhibit booklet, vaudeville sketches staged at the exhibit's openings and scholarly studies from the panel presentations at these openings. Also included are interviews with two major figures in today's Chicano theatre: Luis Valdez and Rodrigo Duarte.

It is hoped that the works included in this volume, as in the exhibit itself, will provide a sense of the breadth and richness of the theatrical past and present of Mexican Americans and other Hispanic artists that have performed for almost two centuries in the Southwest. Above all, we have attempted to provide a sense of continuity in the artistry as well as the social, moral and political functions of creating theatre within the context of a community that exists within a larger, dominating cultural structure that alternates between ignoring and opposing the language, traditions and art forms of the former.

Mexican American Theatre: Then and Now is especially dedicated to those professional artists who experienced the transition from a vibrant and flourishing theatre to all but demise, and then, in their waning years, a rebirth among the youth of what has come to be known as Chicano theatre.

Leonardo García Astol

Monólogo

(Grabado 7 de marzo, 1982,
en el Instituto de Cultura Tejana, San Antonio)

Mi bisabuelo fue un hombre muy valiente. Ustedes no están para creerlo. El vivía por estos rincones. Hace muchísimos años cuando esto estaba plateado de indios . . . eran puros indios. Entonces se hacían los fuertes para defenderse de ellos. Y mi bisabuelo era soldado y el general lo puso en el fuerte y le dijo—Si tenemos que salir, tú te vas a quedar cuidando el fuerte . . . aquí, sin menearte, con tu fusil.

—Sí, mi general.

Se fueron y mi abuelo se quedó solo . . . cuando va llegando una parvada de indios. Mi abuelo . . . quieto . . . quieto . . . no hacía nada, nada. Y habían dado la orden que aquí estaba. Uno de los indios se acercó y con un machete . . . ¡Zás! le cortó la cabeza. La cabeza cayó al arroyo. Mi abuelo decía . . . ¡cará! . . . ¡cará! Pues, a tientas se hincó, a tientas . . . buscó la cabeza. La encontró . . . y de despedida le dio un beso.

Ustedes me van a preguntar, ¿Pero con qué le daba el beso a la cabeza? Pues . . . ¡con la boca del estómago!

¡Y eso no fue nada! Mi padre, ése sí que fue valiente. Mi padre estaba en un teatro, un salón de teatro chico, pero el teatro estaba lleno, repleto de gente, cuando de repente se empezó un incendio. Las llamas empezaron a subir. La gente desesperada corría atropellándose unos a los otros, los niños por el suelo, las mujeres gritando . . . y mi padre se subió al foro, al escenario, y se detuvo diciéndoles—¡Calma, señores, calma! No pasa nada. ¡Vuelvan todos a sus asientos! La gente regresó y, gracias a mi padre, se murieron quemados todos.

Leonardo y Susie Astol / Mateo y Belia Camargo

El Rajá

(Grabado el 7 de marzo, 1982,
en el Instituto de Cultura Tejana, San Antonio)

LALO: ¡Qué barbaridad! ¡Tantos años sin verte ya!

MATEO: Pos aquí me mira, compadre.

LALO: Lo lógico es que no nos hayamos visto porque yo he andado viajando mucho.

MATEO: Con razón no lo había visto, compadre.

LALO: Pues, sí.

MATEO: ¡Qué barbaridad! ¿A dónde fue?

LALO: Uh . . . recorrí casi todo el mundo.

MATEO: Sí, ¿de veras . . . de veras? ¿Fue a Potí?

LALO: ¿Cómo?

MATEO: ¿A Potí?

LALO: ¿Eso queda en Europa?

MATEO: No sé ni dónde está Potí.

LALO: Fui a la India.

MATEO: ¿A la India?

LALO: A la India.

MATEO: ¿Y qué vio allá?

LALO: Oh, vi una de indios y una de indias . . . No, pero me presentaron al mero mero, al Rajá.

MATEO: ¿Al qué?

LALO: Al Rajá.

MATEO: ¿Al Rajá?

LALO: De la India. Sí, ése fue el rey . . . y al Califa también, también, quien me presentó inmediatamente a su señora.

MATEO: ¿A la esposa del Rajá?

LALO: ¿La Rajá? Bueno, sí. Además, me presentó a sus hijitos.

MATEO: ¿Esos cómo se llaman?

LALO: Los Rajoncitos. Le caí tan bien, tan bien, que me hizo un regalo maravilloso. Ya con ese regalo yo no necesito nada en el mundo.

MATEO: ¿De veras?

LALO: Sí. Aquí lo traigo. Se lo voy a enseñar. Mira lo que me regaló.

MATEO: Ah, eso . . . ¡es una flor!

LALO: ¡No, no, no! Pero es una flor mágica.

MATEO: ¿Mágica?

LALO: Sí, es mágica . . .

MATEO: ¿Es mágica esa cosa?

LALO: Esta flor se la da a oler a cualquiera, a cualquier mujer. Nada más se la da usted a oler y cae rediviva a sus pies . . .

MATEO: ¿Es verdad?

LALO: La mera verdad.

MATEO: ¡Eso no existe . . . !

LALO: Aquí tengo la prueba. Mira, aquí viene una. La voy a probar . . . a ver . . . a ver . . . Buenas tardes.

SUSIE: Buenas tardes.

LALO: Oiga, señorita . . .

SUSIE: Diga . . .

LALO: ¿Le han dicho que es usted muy bonita?

SUSIE: Oiga, ¡¿cómo se atreve usted?! Le voy a llamar a mi marido, ¡eh! para que luego . . .

LALO: ¿Está casada?

SUSIE: Pues, ¿no lo ve?

LALO: No me importa. ¡Yo la quiero!

SUSIE: Bueno . . . ¿Qué es lo que quiere usted?

LALO: Yo la quiero (De rodillas y buscando la flor sin encontrarla).

SUSIE: Además, usted no me gusta . . . parece perro sentado.

MATEO: ¡Ay, éste . . . mujeriego, y que la magia y quién sabe qué! ¿Qué pasó?

LALO: Ah, no se la di a oler. ¿Quién sabe dónde la tenía yo?

MATEO: Entonces, ¿cómo vas a demostrar que esta flor así tiene el . . .

LALO: Ahí viene . . . ahí viene . . .

MATEO: A ver . . . a ver . . .

SUSIE: ¿Otra vez usted?

LALO: (Pasa la flor bajo las narices de Susie.) Por lo que me dijo usted hace un momento . . .

SUSIE: ¡Qué bonito me siento! ¡Ay! (Lo abraza.) ¡Ay, mi Jorge Rivero! ¡Ay, qué lindo!

MATEO: ¡No lo puedo creer!

LALO: Pues, ¿no lo vio con sus propios ojos?

MATEO: ¡Qué barbaridad! ¡Es maravilloso! ¡Caray! Oiga, compadre, se la voy a pedir prestada. A mí me va muy mal con todas las mujeres.

LALO: ¿Le va mal?

MATEO: Pero mal. Yo no tengo suerte. Me ven y hasta la espalda me dan. Voy a un restorán y ni caso me hacen. Ninguna mesera viene a atenderme y . . .

LALO: ¡Ya ya ya ya! No sigas diciéndome tanto que me va a hacer llorar.

MATEO: ¿Me la prestas compadre? (Lalo se la da.) Mira, ahí viene una

. . .

BELIA: *(Cantando.)* La, la, la . . .

MATEO: Señorita . . .

BELIA: *(Espantada y gritando.)* ¡Ay! ¡No me digas eso a mí! ¿Qué hay? ¿Qué quiere?

LALO: Oh, ¡qué susto me dio!

MATEO: Oiga, . . . agarra mi corazón, para que veas . . . bum, bum, bum. *(Le coloca la mano sobre su corazón.)*

BELIA: Ese tico-tico, tico-tico no es corazón, es otra cosa . . .

MATEO: Fíjese que . . .

BELIA: ¡Fíjese que nada! Usted no tiene derecho a hablarme a mí. Yo vengo muy tranquila por la calle . . . *(Mateo va a hablar y Belia le pega.)* ¡Cállese el hocico!

MATEO: ¡No!

BELIA: ¡Trapón! ¡Chaparro! *(Gritan y discuten los dos.)*

MATEO: Oiga, oiga, fíjese que yo quisiera decirle algo.

BELIA: *(Sigue gritando y Mateo le pasa la flor por sus narices.)* ¡Ay! *(Suave.)* ¿Dónde estoy? ¡Ay! pero, ¿qué es esto? ¡Sylvester Stallone! ¡Qué machote! ¡Papasote! *(Sale.)*

MATEO: ¡Qué emoción! ¡Qué barbaridad! ¡Hasta que una mujer me hizo caso!

LALO: Con esa flor . . . cualquiera . . . nada más.

MATEO: Fíjese, qué maravilloso, qué barbaridad . . . y pensar que lo único que hay que hacer es pasársela *(La pasa por la cara de Lalo.)* por las narices.

LALO: ¡Qué elegante, papá! *(Le abraza muy afeminado y el otro le huye. Salen.)*

Leonardo García Astol and Susie Astol

La viajera mundial

(Grabado en el Auditorio del Inmaculado Corazón de María, San Antonio, Noviembre 1982.)

Escena: En la calle.

LALO: ¡Susie!

SUSIE: ¡Lalo! ¡No hombre!

LALO: ¡Qué barbaridad!

SUSIE: ¡Ay, mira no más! ¡Tanto tiempo sin vernos! *(Se abrazan.)*

LALO: Pero años y años que no nos veíamos. ¿Qué ha sido tu vida?

SUSIE: ¿Mi vida?

LALO: Sí.

SUSIE: Pues, mi vida ha sido, Lalo, viajar.

LALO: ¿Viajar?

SUSIE: Sí.

LALO: Siempre te gustó mucho viajar.

SUSIE: Tú sabes que siempre he sido aficonada a la pesca.

LALO: ¿A la pesca?

SUSIE: Sí.

LALO: Ah sí, me acuerdo de que siempre quierías pescarme a mí, pero
 . . . no . . .

SUSIE: ¡Déjate de bromas! No, hombre, como a mí me gusta viajar, fui a
 la China.

LALO: ¿A la China?

SUSIE: Sí.

LALO: Bueno, ¿fuiste o te mandaron?

SUSIE: No, fui. Fui a la China. Y me recomendaron de un lago precioso
 que había allí para pescar. ¿Y sabes lo que hice?

LALO: No.

SUSIE: Fui a mi casa, saqué mi caña, le puse el anzuelo y le puse la
 carnada y lo arrojé así *(Señala con el brazo.)* al lago y así estaba,
 mira, zás, zás, zás *(Haciendo como pescando.)* y, el brazo, cada vez
 que hacía así, era un pescado . . . En menos de media hora junté mil
 pescados.

LALO: ¡No . . . no . . . no!

SUSIE: ¿Cómo que no?

LALO: ¿Para eso te fuiste hasta la China?

SUSIE: Pues, sí, claro que sí, y me voy a volver a ir.

LALO: Pues, qué tonta eres. Porque aquí, aquí en San Antonio, sin
 ir más lejos, el Arroyo del Alazán . . . una cosa preciosa . . . mira,

el otro día iba yo pasando por ahí y se me antojó pescar y me acordé que no llevaba yo nada: caña, anzuelo, ni carnada, no llevaba nada.

SUSIE: ¿Y qué hiciste?

LALO: Me arremangué la manga de la camisa, metí la mano al agua . . . ¡nada! La volví a meter . . . y ¡nada! Otra vez . . . y nada . . . y nada.

SUSIE: ¿Y nada?

LALO: Nada.

SUSIE: ¿Y qué?

LALO: Nada de agua, puro pescado.

SUSIE: ¡Válgame Dios! Ay qué Lalo, tú sigues con tus bromitas.

LALO: Bueno, ¿y a dónde más fuiste?

SUSIE: Bueno, te voy a decir que fui a la India . . . porque me recomendaron que fuera a ver un cerro . . . que es el cerro más alto que hay, creo que de todo el mundo . . .

LALO: ¿El más alto?

SUSIE: Sí, y ese cerro, cuando tú dices una palabra, te la contesta.

LALO: Ah . . . ¿tiene eco?

SUSIE: Tiene eco. Y fui así, le dije "Cafeee . . ." y me contesto "café, café, café, café, café, café" . . . así estuvo por mucho rato.

LALO: No sirve.

SUSIE: ¿Cómo que no sirve?

LALO: ¡Claro que no! ¿Para qué ir a la India? Aquí, saliendo de San Antonio, ahí cerquita de Potí, hay un cerrazo . . . bueno, no es tan grande, más bien es un cerrito chiquito y tiene un eco bárbaro.

SUSIE: ¿De veras?

LALO: De veras. Y fíjate, que yo fui y paré como tú . . . le dije "café" . . .

SUSIE: ¿Y qué te contestó?

LALO: "¿Con leche o sin leche?"

SUSIE: ¡Ay, Lalo!

LALO: Oye, supe que también fuiste a Chicago.

SUSIE: Ay, sí, me fui a Chicago. Me fui a divertir.

LALO: Pues, ¿qué hiciste allá en Chicago?

SUSIE: Me fui porque quería tener un diploma de algo.

LALO: ¿Ah, sí?

SUSIE: De algo que me graduara.

LALO: ¿Para qué estudiaste?

SUSIE: Te vas a asustar.

LALO: No, hombre, ¿Por qué? ¿Ingeniera?

SUSIE: No.

LALO: ¿Abogada?

SUSIE: No.

LALO: ¿Doctora?

SUSIE: No.

LALO: ¿Entonces?

SUSIE: ¡Ratera!

LALO: ¿Qué?

SUSIE: Sí, de ratera.

LALO: ¿Fuiste para estudiar para ratera?

SUSIE: Sí, fui a estudiar . . .

LALO: Pues, ¿para eso se estudia?

SUSIE: Sí, tienes que saber cómo sacar las carteras a las personas . . . así sacar las bolsas . . .

LALO: Bueno, ¿cómo le hiciste? A ver, cuéntame.

SUSIE: Bueno, me dieron una clase . . . una clase muy rara, pero una clase. Allí había un *hall* muy largo a allí en el *hall* había un maniquí . . .

LALO: ¿Un muñeco?

SUSIE: Sí, un muñeco.

LALO: ¿Tamaño natural?

SUSIE: Tamaño natural de una persona, pues claro.

LALO: Eso es lo que te iba a decir . . . yo no soy natural.

SUSIE: Bueno, y ese maniquí tenía muchas campanitas . . . todo, todo, todo lleno de campanitas. Era la prueba.

LALO: ¿Desde el cuello hasta los pies?

SUSIE: Desde el cuello hasta los pies. Y entonces le pusieron una cartera aquí (*Metiendo la mano hasta el bolsillo interior del saco de Lalo.*) . . . al maniquí . . . y yo tenía que ir con mucho cuidado . . . era la prueba para que me graduara . . . sabes lo nerviosa que soy . . .

LALO: . . . a que no sonara ni una campanita.

SUSIE: A que no sonara ni una, porque si suena, no . . . Fui y le saqué la cartera y no sonaron las campanitas. Así que me gradué.

LALO: No, si tienes una cara de ratera que no puedes con ella.

SUSIE: ¿De veras?

LALO: Bueno, y no te quito más tiempo. Tengo que irme.

SUSIE: Yo también. (*Los dos hacen como si se van y de repente se detienen.*) Oye, Lalo, ¿queres hacerme el favor de decirme la hora?

LALO: Sí, ¿cómo no? Oye, ¡mi reloj! ¡mi reloj!

SUSIE: Pues, ¿tu reloj? Mira, aquí lo tengo. Para que veas que soy una gran ratera.

LALO: ¡Mira, nada más! Ahora me he convencido que eres una gran ratera.

SUSIE: Bueno, *bye bye*.

LALO: Espera un tantito. ¿y tú no sientes nada?

SUSIE: ¿De qué?

LALO: Pues, de algo.

SUSIE: No siento nada.

LALO: Pues, mira, cuando te abracé, tú no te diste cuenta y . . . te quité esto (*Saca un brassiere del bolsillo y se lo enseña.*)

El Fotógrafo

*El fotógrafo ocupado en limpiar su máquina fotográfica (una caja
grande al estilo antiguo):*

FOTOGRAFO: ¡Ay! Pero un día. . . *(Hablando con un cliente imaginario.)*
Dígame. Sí, yo soy el famoso fotógrafo Julián Masacate . . . y usted
es la actriz Flora de Aguascalientes. ¡Su última película fue fabulosa!
¡Magnífica! ¿Pero qué hace usted aquí? ¡Oh! ¡Una foto? Pero, cómo
no, si aquí estoy para servirle . . . *(Aparte a su secretaria.)* Secretaria
Sofía por favor, a cancelar todas las citas para hoy. ¿Qué? ¡Sí! ¡Claro!
Que se espere el gobernador hasta mañana. Ah . . . Señorita Flora de
Aguascalientes, por favor, siéntese, yo . . . *(Tocan a la puerta.)*
¡Perdón! *(Tocan de nuevo y el fotógrafo deja su fantasía.)* ¡Ay! ¡Un
día . . . ! Ay voy, ay voy. ¡Pasen! ¡Pasen! *(Entran Madre e Hija.)*
MADRE: Buenos días.
FOTOGRAFO: Buenos días. ¿En qué le puedo servir?
MADRE: Gustaría una foto de mi hijita Lucita. *(Lucita lamiendo una
paleta gigantesca.)*
FOTOGRAFO: Buenos días, Lucita.
LUCITA: . . .
FOTOGRAFO: Por favor, tome asiento, Lucita. *(Se sienta.)* Muy bien.
¡Qué bonita su hija!
MADRE: Gracias. *(Saca su espejo de su bolsa y comienza a arreglarse.)*
FOTOGRAFO: *(Debajo de la cortina de la máquina fotográfica.)* Lucitaa,
Lucitaa . . . por favor, mira para acá. ¡Lucita! Señora, su hija, por
favor. *(Lucita vuelve hacia la máquina y la mira.)*
MADRE: ¿Qué tiene?
FOTOGRAFO: *(Sorprendido.)* Nada . . . gracias. *(Se mete debajo de la
cortina de nuevo y Lucita se cubre la cara con la paleta.)* Lucitaa,
Lucitaa . . . *(Deja la máquina y se acerca a Lucita.)* Dame el dulce,
¿sí? *(Asiente con su cabeza.)* Por favor . . . *(Asiente con su cabeza.)*
Señora . . . su hija . . . *(Lucita le pone el dulce de la paleta, toda
lamida, en la mano del Fotógrafo.)*
MADRE: ¡Qué tiene mi hija?
FOTOGRAFO: Nada, gracias. *(Regresa a la máquina.)* Lucita . . . una
sonrisa . . . por favor . . . Sí . . . una sonrisa para la foto . . . ¡Señora,
su hija!
MADRE: ¿Qué? *(Se sonríe Lucita revelando la ausencia de muchos*

dientes.)

FOTOGRAFO: Nada. *(Comienza a reírse.)*

MADRE: ¿De qué se ríe?

FOTOGRAFO: Oh nada, señora, nada. *(Lucita le muerde la mano.)* ¡Ay! ¡Qué bonita su hija? *(Se coloca detrás de la máquina de nuevo y saca un pajarito.)* Lucita, mira el pajarito . . . el pajaritooo! *(Deja la máquina y se acerca a la madre.)* Señora, su hija . . . *(Lucita saca unas tijeras y se corta el cordón del pajarito.)*

MADRE: ¿Mi hija? ¿Qué tiene mi hija?

FOTOGRAFO: No quiere ver el pajarito.

MADRE: ¡Cuál pajarito!

FOTOGRAFO: Este pajarito . . . *(Ve el palo con cordón sin pajarito . . .)* Nada, senóra, nada. Qué bonita eres, Lucita. Lucitaaa . . . Mira, por arriba . . . ¡Come saliva! *(Comienza a reírse, pero se para al ver a la Madre.)*

LUCITA: Señor Fotógrafo . . . mire pa' abajo . . . ¡Come gargajo! *(La Madre y la Hija se ríen.)*

FOTOGRAFO: *(Debajo de la cortina.)* One more time! Lucita . . . *(Tocan a la puerta.)* Con permiso. *(Sale para contestar la puerta.)*

MADRE: Ay, Lucita, qué bonita eres.

LUCITA: Gracias, Mamá.

MADRE: *(Va y se coloca debajo de la máquina para ver a su Hija.)* ¿Cómo se . . .

FOTOGRAFO: *(Regresa y levanta la falda de la Madre creyendo que es la cortina de la caja fotográfica.)* No, dile que mañana . . . ¡Ay! *(Alboroto completo, salen corriendo.)*

Two Centuries of
Hispanic Theatre
in the Southwest

*A Multi-Media Show on the
History of Hispanic Theatre in the Southwest*

1982

Two Centuries of Hispanic Theatre in the Southwest

Nicolás Kanellos
Project Director

Francisco Blasco
Project Coordinator

Awilda Córdova
Business Manager

Cristelia Pérez
Administrative Secretary

Betti Maldonado-Martínez
Nelson Martínez
Producers of Exhibit Video Tape

Exhibit Schedule

Two Centuries of Hispanic Theatre in the Southwest

by Nicolás Kanellos

The first European-type dramatic performance north of the Río Grande River took place somewhere near El Paso in 1598 when Juan de Oñate's men improvised a play based on their adventures in exploring New Mexico. From that time on, folk dramas of varying description—from shepherd's plays *(pastorelas)* and heroic dramas like *Moros y cristianos, Los tejanos* and *Los camanches* to farmworker skits—have been important rituals and pastimes for Spanish-speakers of the Southwest. Theatre has always been so essential to Hispanic culture as a form of expression, cultural preservation, and, of course, just entertainment, that even before the Mexican American War, professional and semi-professional theatres began to appear in the Southwest. California port cities, successful trade centers that were easily accessible to Mexico by steamship, became entertainment centers which supported theatrical productions in the Spanish language.

By the 1840s, both professionals and amateurs were staging plays in the Monterey area and Los Angeles. These plays were staged as entertainment for both Spanish and English speakers. Such productions as that of *Morayma*, (a melodrama inspired in a Christian-Moorish romance of Medieval Spain), reviewed by the *Californian* on October 6, 1847, were produced for private subscription in Monterey in the billiard parlor of an inn. By the 1840s, Los Angeles' Hispanic community housed its productions in a theatre in which, according to *Golden Era* columnist, J. E. Lawrence, "the Mexicans and the native Californians of the place amused themselves." On July 4, 1848, however, Don Antonio F. Coronel, future mayor of Los Angeles, opened another theatre, as an addition to his home; it included a covered stage with a proscenium, and housed productions in Spanish and English. From 1852 to 1854, Don Vicente Guerrero's Union Theatre housed legitimate drama in Spanish, directed by Guerrero himself on Saturday and Sunday evenings. Two other early theatres that housed productions in Spanish and English were Stearn's Hall, opened in 1859 by the very Hispanicized Don Abel Stearns, and Temple Hall, which existed from 1859 to 1892. In the 1860s and 1870s, the Hispanic community also frequented the Merced Theatre (still standing today), Teatro Alarcón and Turn Verein Hall.

Los Angeles' Temple Hall.

San Antonio and El Paso, far inland and not as accessible to trade and the arts in the mid-nineteenth century, did not develop a Hispanic stage as quickly as did the California port cities. It seems that as late as 1856 San Antonio did not have a theatre house. An editorial published on July 9, 1856, in San Antonio's newspaper, *El Bejareño*, indicates that some young people in the community wanted to construct a theatre, but the editorial argued that the funds could be used better for a hospital, which the city also needed. During the same year, however, *El Bejareño* (June 21 and July 19) reported on Mexican circuses touring locally. It is probable, however, that touring professional companies were playing in Texas at this time, although not in theatre houses. In Laredo as late as 1891, theatrical performances were staged in the open market or at taverns for what the newspaper, *El Correo de Laredo* (July 22, 1891), called "gente *non sancta*" or "unholy people."

On the other hand, the professional stage in California had become so established and important to the Spanish-speaking community, that by the 1860s theatre companies that once toured Mexico, settled down to serve as repertory companies, choosing Los Angeles and San Francisco as their home bases. Such was the case of La Familia Estrella, under the directorship of the great Mexican leading man, Gerardo López del

Primer Actor Gerardo López del Castillo.

Castillo. The company was typical of those that toured Mexico in that it was composed of Mexican and Spanish players, staged Spanish melodrama and occasionally a Mexican or a Cuban play, and held most of its performances on Sunday evenings. The program was a complete evening's entertainment that included a three or four-act drama, song and dance, and a one-act farce or comic dialog to close the performance. The full-length plays that were the heart of the program were mostly melodramas by Spanish authors like Zorrilla, Larra and Bretón de los Herreros and, for the most part, represent texts which were readily available then and now.

Besides carrying on his regular professional activities as an actor and director, López del Castillo was deeply involved in community and patriotic affairs, and some of the troupe's performances helped raise funds for Zaragoza's and Juárez's liberation forces during the Franco-

Los Angeles' Merced Theatre.

Mexican War. He also served as President of San Francisco's Junta Patriótica Mexicana. López del Castillo's nationalism and community involvement represent the first example of the kind of social responsibility that would characterize Hispanic theatre in the communities of the Southwest, even up to the present.

While San Francisco became the home base of the Familia Estrella company, it did tour as well along a circuit including travel by steamship to Los Angeles and Mazatlán and inland in northern Mexico and up to Tucson by stagecoach. The troupe's success seems to have been as great in Los Angeles as in San Francisco, judging from the favorable reviews written, even in the English-language media. *The Los Angeles News*, February 27, 1867, accorded Amalia Estrella del Castillo this favorable comment:

> Señora Estrella del Castillo took . . . the difficult role of "María" in *Troubadour* which she played with happy effect, her rich voice adding greatly to the natural beauty of the piece in the song, "Grace of God." In this piece, Señora Castillo exhibited genuine talent in all parts of the play, successively as a shepherdess, dancing girl, accomplished young lady of the world, and a maniac bereft of reason.

Appreciation of the other great leading-lady of the time, Laura Morales de Mollá, was also strong, as can be seen from this poem

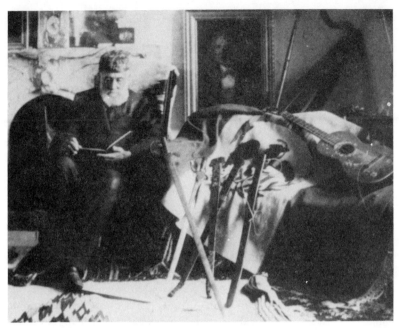

Don Antonio F. Coronel.

dedicated to her by theatre-owner, Don Antonio F. Coronel (my translation):

> Oh, bewitching Laura, who taught you
> to make us enjoy such serene happiness?
> Who granted you the delicate artistry
> in which you make us laugh and sigh?
> From whom, moving free on stage,
> have you learned to move us to piety,
> and after storming hard and furiously,
> whisper the name of your loves?
> You make happy or you sadden, as you please;
> you inflame passions, as you please;
> you move, calm, agitate, harden,
> and melt all tender hearts.
> Whoever hears you with sensitivity appreciates
> the prodigiousness of your marvellous art,
> becomes ecstatic, is delighted, is fooled,
> and enjoys the sweetest repose.
>
> (Los Angeles, June 21, 1883.)

Of the seven, known professional companies that performed in the Los Angeles-San Francisco area during the 1860s to the 1870s, the two with the greatest longevity seem to have been the José Pérez Company and the Compañía Española de Angel Mollá, both of which also toured along the Los Angeles-northern Mexico-Tucson circuit. In 1876 the Pérez company came under the directorship of Pedro C. de Pellón and seems to have disappeared from the Los Angeles area. Pellón reappears again in 1878 in Tucson where he organized the town's first group of amateur actors at the Teatro Recreo. Mollá's company, on the other hand, continued to tour to Tucson until 1882. Tucson's early Hispanic theatre was soon eclipsed, however, with the arrival of rail transportation and tours by English-language companies from the East.

By the turn of the century, major Spanish-language companies were performing all along the Mexico-United States border, following a circuit that extended from Laredo to San Antonio and El Paso and through New Mexico and Arizona to Los Angeles, then up to San Francisco or down to San Diego. The advent of rail transportation and the automobile make theatre more accessible to smaller population centers. Tent theatres and smaller make-shift companies performed along the Río Grande Valley, only occasionally venturing into the big cities to compete with the major drama and *zarzuela* companies. By 1910 a few of the smaller cities, like Laredo, even supported their own repertory companies. Theatrical activities expanded rapidly, even boomed, when thousands of immigrants fled the Mexican Revolution and settled in the United States from the border states all the way up to the Midwest. During the decades of the Revolution, many of Mexico's greatest artists and their theatrical companies were to take up temporary residence in the United States; however, some would never return to their homeland.

Mexican and Spanish companies, and an occasional Cuban, Argentine or other Hispanic troupe, began to tour throughout the Southwest and as far north and east as New York, where there was also a lively Hispanic theatrical tradition. Some companies even made the coast-to-coast tour via the northern route: New York, Philadelphia, Cleveland, Chicago, and points west to Los Angeles. The company of the famed Mexican actress, Virginia Fábregas, was of particular importance in its frequent tours, because it not only performed the latest works from the theatres of Mexico City and Madrid, but some of its actors left the companies during United States tours to form their own troupes here. Also La Fábregas encouraged the development of local playwrights in Los Angeles by buying the rights to their works and performing them on tour. The Spanish companies of María Guerrero and Gregorio Martínez Sierra also made the coast-to-coast jaunts, assisted by New York booking agents and established theatrical circuits. When

SRA. VIRGINIA FABREGAS, distinguida Primera Actriz Mexicana,
que celebra su función de beneficio y despedida en el Lyceum Hall, la noche
el Martes 31 de Dicimbre.

vaudeville became popular in the twenties and thirties, the Mexican performers, many of whom previously starred in high drama and *zarzuela,* toured not only the Hispanic but the American vaudeville circuits and even performed actively in Canada.

It should also be noted that many companies offered a variety of theatrical genres from *zarzuela* and operetta to drama, *comedia, revista* and *variedades.* As the hundreds of companies throughout the Southwest adapted to changing tastes and economic conditions, the shifting of repertoires and the recruitment of new casts and musicians eventually brought about companies that could perform virtually anything, complementing a film with variety acts in the afternoon, producing a full-length drama in the evening, a *zarzuela* and a drama on Saturday and Sunday, different works each day, of course.

The two cities with the largest Mexican populations, Los Angeles and San Antonio, naturally became theatrical centers, the former also feeding off of the important film industry in Hollywood. In fact, Los Angeles became a manpower pool for Hispanic theatre. Actors, directors, technicians and musicians from throughout the Southwest and even New York were drawn here looking for employment in the theatre

25

María Teresa Montoya in Los Angeles, 1922.

Los Angeles' California Theatre today.

arts industry. Both Los Angeles and San Antonio went through a period
of intense expansion and building of theatrical facilities in the late teens
and early twenties. San Antonio's most important house was the Teatro
Nacional built in 1917 and owned by Sam Lucchese, also owner of the
Zendejas and other theatres in Laredo. Other San Antonio theatres
were the Aurora, Texas, Obrero, Azteca, Hidalgo, Zaragoza, Princess,
Unión, Amigos del Pueblo, Salón Casino, Beethoven Hall, Majestic,
Municipal Auditorium, Progreso, Palace, Teatro Salón San Fernando,
Juárez, State. Los Angeles was able to support five major Hispanic
theatre houses with programs that changed daily from 1918 until the
early 1930s. The theatres and their peak years were Teatro Hidalgo
(1918-1934), Teatro México (1921-1933), Teatro Capitol (1924-1926),
Teatro Zendejas later Novel (1919-1924) and Teatro Principal (1921-1929).
Four other theatres—Prince (1922-1926), California (1927-1934), Cali-
fornia International (1930-1932) and Estela (1930-1932)—were also
important, and at least thirteen others housed professional companies
on a more irregular basis between 1915 and 1935. These were the
Metropolitan, Cabaret Sanromán, Lyseum Hall, Empress, Leo Carillo,
Orange Grove, Mason, Million Dollar, Major, Paramount, Figueroa
Playhouse, Alcázar, Philharmonic Auditorium and Unique.

   While it is true that in the Southwest, as in Mexico, Spanish drama
and *zarzuela* dominated the stage up to the early twenties, the clamor
for plays written by Mexican writers had increased to such an extent that
by 1923 Los Angeles had become a center for Mexican play-writing
probably unparalleled in the history of Hispanic communities in the

Gabriel Navarro.

United States. While continuing to consume plays by Spanish authors like Benavente, Echegaray, Martínez-Sierra, Linares Rivas and the Quintero Brothers, the theatres and communities encouraged local writing by offering cash prizes in contests, lucrative contracts and lavish productions. As the local writers became more well known, the popularity of their works brought record attendance into the theatre houses.

It was often repeated in the newspapers that the Hispanic theatres drew their largest crowds every time they featured plays by local writers. For instance, Gabriel Navarro wrote in *La Opinión*, April 12, 1930, that the largest profits of 1929 were made at the Teatro México from local plays. Nevertheless, as popular as these plays may have been, business interests at times worked against their production and against the playwrights' enjoying the benefits of their craft. According to Esteban V. Escalante, *La Opinión*, April 20, 1930, the writer's 25% share of the opening-day box office—which often amounted to $100 to $150—led impresarios to jealously limit the author's payment to a flat fee of $20 or $30 or simply to eliminate local plays and produce instead well-worn *obras* for which they did not have to pay a dime.

Popular Los Angeles comedian and theatrical director, Romualdo Tirado.

The period from 1922 to 1933 saw the emergence and box-office success of a group of playwrights in Los Angeles that was made up mainly of Mexican theatrical expatriates and newspapermen. At the center of the group were four playwrights whose works not only filled the theatres on Los Angeles' Main Street, but were also contracted throughout the Southwest and Mexico: Eduardo Carrillo, an actor; Adalberto Elías González, a novelist; Esteban V. Escalante, a newspaperman and theatrical director; and Gabriel Navarro, poet, novelist, orchestra director, columnist for *La Opinión* and editor of *La Revista de los Angeles*. There were at least twenty other locally residing writers who saw their works produced on the professional stage, not to mention the scores of authors of *revistas* that dealt with local and current themes for the Mexican companies that presented a different program each day. A few of the most productive and popular authors of *revistas* were: Don Catarino, los Sandozequi, and Guz Aguila (Antonio Guzmán Aguilera). Guzmán Aguilera, famous in Mexico as an *autor de revistas*, held the distinction of being under contract to the Teatro Hidalgo in Los Angeles for the extraordinary amount of $1000 per month.

The Los Angeles writers were serving a public that was hungry to see itself reflected on stage, an audience whose interest was piqued by

29

Beatriz "La Chata" Noloesca and Pedro "Ramirín" González González.

plays relating to current events, politics, sensational crimes and, of course, the real-life epic of a people living under the cultural and economic domination of an English-speaking, American society on land that was once part of Mexican patrimony. Of course the *revistas* kept the social and political criticism directed at both the United States and Mexico within the lighter context of music and humor in such pieces as Antonio Guzmán Aguilera's *Mexico para los mexicanos* and *Los Angeles vacilador;* Daniel Venegas' *El con-su-lado* and *Maldito jazz;* Brígido Caro's *Mexico y Estados Unidos,* Gabriel Navarro's *La ciudad de irás y no volverás;* Raúl Castell's *El mundo de las pelonas* and *En el país del Shimmy;* and *Los efectos de la crisis, Regreso a mi tierra, Los repatriados, Whiskey, morfina y marihuana* and *El desterrado,* to mention just a few of the *revistas* of Don Catarino, who often played the role of the *pelado* in these works.

Don Fito, the *peladito* of the Carpa García.

It is in the *revistas* that we find a great deal of humor based on culture shock typically derived from following the misadventures of a naive, recent immigrant from Mexico who has difficulty getting accustomed to life in the big Anglo-American metropolis. It is also in the *revista* that the raggedly dressed underdog, the *pelado,* comes to the fore with his low-class dialect and acerbic satire. A forerunner of characters like Cantinflas, the *pelado* really develops in the humble *carpa,* or tent show, that evolved in Mexico and existed in the Southwest of the United States until the 1950s. One theatre critic has said of the *pelado* that his improvised dialog "brings to the scene the fine humor of the people, their critical spirit, their complaints and desires; and the people, in turn, upon seeing their own existence portrayed on stage, cooperate directly with the comics, conversing with them, with crude

Don Suave and Don Lalo.

sincerity." Although the *pelado* was often criticized for his low humor and scandalous language, critics today consider the character to be a genuine and authentic Mexican contribution to the history of theatre.

Characters like Don Lalo (Leonardo García Astol), the comic hobo of the "Don Lalo y Don Suave" vaudeville sketches, owes a great deal to the *carpas* and the *pelado*. The same is true of "El Niño Fidencio" (Francisco Vega) in the Los Angeles theatre of the 1930s.

The more serious, full-length plays addressed the situation of Mexicans in California on a broader, more epic scale, often in plays based on the history of the Mexican-Anglo struggle in California. Brígido Caro's *Joaquín Murrieta*, the tale of the California bandit during the Gold Rush days, not only achieved success on the professional stage, but was also adopted by the community for political and cultural fund-raising activities. Such groups as the Cuadro de Aficionados Junípero Serra performed this play to raise funds for organizations like the Alianza Hispano Americana. Eduardo Carrillo's *El proceso de Aurelio Pompa* dealt with the unjust trial and sentencing of a Mexican immigrant and also was performed for fund raising purposes in the community. Esteban

Adalberto Elías González.

V. Escalante's pieces, however, were more sentimental and usually written in a one-act format. Gabriel Navarro also developed one-act pieces, but in a more satirical and humoristic vein. But his full-length dramas, *Los emigrados* and *El sacrificio* again dealt with the epic of Mexicans in California, the latter play with a setting in 1846.

By far the most prolific and respected of the Los Angeles playwrights was Adalberto Elías González, some of whose works were not only performed locally, but throughout the Southwest and Mexico, were made into movies and translated into English. His works that were produced in Los Angeles ran the gamut from historical drama to dime-novel sensationalism. The most famous of his plays, *Los amores de Ramona*, a stage adaptation of Helen Hunt Jackson's California novel, *Ramona; A Story*, broke all box-office records when it was seen by more than fifteen thousand people after only eight performances.

In truth it must be stated that the greater part of theatrical fare served purely entertainment and cultural purposes, while obliquely contributing to the expatriate community's solidarity within the context of the larger, English-speaking society. The majority of the plays pro-

Circo Escalante Hnos.

COMPAÑIA DE BAILE Y VARIEDADES

Carpas Situadas en el extremo oeste de la calle Congress

Hoy-Martes 29 de Marzo-Hoy

Regia Funcion de Gracia --- Notable Acontecimiento

LO MEJOR DE LO MEJOR

Funcion de Beneficio

Predomina la Nobleza, Predomina el Humanitarismo

¡Ojo!   ¡Ojo!   ¡Ojo!

AL PUBLICO

Habiendo acordado el comité "Grijalva" el que encargado esta parte colectar fondos de la hospitalaria colonia mexicana, con objeto de llevar hasta el fin la defensa judicial de un hermano de raza, ha ocurrido, repito, á la compañia Escalante Hnos., solicitando encarecidamente, de dicha empresa, una funcion de gracia, funcion de beneficio, para favorecer mas los fondos destinados a tan noble y humanitaria accion. los hermanos Escalante, sin poner objeción alguna, gustosos y satisfechos de tan digno proceder, han accedido orgullosos de poder contribuir con su pequeño granito de arena y al mismo tiempo cumplir con un deber sagrado.

Esperamos del amable y benévolo público que nos favorezca, ocurran a esta simpatica velada que tiene por objeto tan noble y magnánimo principio, un dúa mas que el público favorecedor siempre se ha distinguido por su caritativo proceder, y por lo mismo, recordamos no olvidar que tan enorme pena puede acabar la vida de una amable esposa y amable hermana la que deja tras si á sufrir inexplicables peripecias. Así tributamos las mas debidas gracias a todo aquel que pudiera prestar una mano ayudadora a quien tanto lo necesita.

ESCALANTE HNOS.   COMITE "GRIJALVA."

ALFREDO GRIJALVA

Trapecios -- Barras -- Alambris-
tas -- Bailes -- Cantos
Couplet, Zarzuela, Recitaciones,
Excentricos y Pantomimas esta
Noche.
No Faltando los Siempre Gracio-
sos y Ocurrentes "Cara Sucia,"
"Tony" y "Chamaco."
Al Circo esta Noche a Contribuir
con tan Noble Cometido

PRECIOS DE ENTRADA

Entrada General	50c
Niños	25c
Asientos Reservados -- Ex	25c

Poster, Circo Escalante.

duced represented the standard fare from the stages of Mexico City and Madrid. However, as can be seen from the above list of plays written and produced in Los Angeles, the playwrights and impresarios did not falter in dealing with controversial material. Many of their plays dealt with the historical and current circumstances of Mexicans in California from a nationalistic and at times political perspective, but always with seriousness and propriety.

The *revistas*, on the other hand, represented a genre that had developed in Mexico as a format for piquant political commentary and grievances were readily articulated in them, fun was poked at both United States and Mexican government, the Mexican Revolution was satirically reconsidered over and over again, and Mexican American culture was contrasted with the "purer" Mexican version. This social and political commentary was carried out despite the fact that both audiences and performers were mostly immigrants, and thus, liable to deportation or repatriation. It must be remembered that the performance language was Spanish and in-group sentiments could easily be expressed, especially through the protection of satire and humor.

It should also be reemphasized that, from the beginning of the Hispanic stage in the Southwest, the relationship of performers and theatres to the community and the nationality was close; the Hispanic stage served to reenforce the sense of community by bringing all Spanish-speakers together in a cultural act: the preservation and the support of the language and the art of Mexicans and other *hispanos* in the face of domination from a foreign culture. Theatre, more than any other art form, became essential to promoting ethnic or national identity and solidifying the colony of expatriates and migrants. Thus, over and above the artistic, within the expatriate Mexican community both professional and amateur theatre took on specific social functions that were hardly ever assumed on the stages of Mexico City.

The professional theatre houses became the temples of culture where the Mexican and Hispanic community as a whole could gather and, in the words of theatre critic, Fidel Murillo, (*La Opinión*, November 20, 1930) "keep the lamp of our culture lighted," regardless of social class, religion or region of origin. A drama critic for San Antonio's *La Prensa*, in the April 26, 1916 edition, underlined the social and nationalistic functions of the theatre: "attending the artistic performances at the Teatro Juárez can be considered a patriotic deed which assists in cultural solidarity in support of a modest group of Mexican actors who are fighting for their livelihood in a foreign land and who introduce us to the most precious jewels of contemporary theatre in our native tongue, that is, the sweet and sonorous language of Cervantes." Thus the theatre became an institution in the Southwest for the preservation of the culture in a foreign environment and for resistance against the influence of the dominant society.

Of course, within the theatre house itself, class distinctions were established by price and location of the seating, and if there were any members of the community that could not afford even the modest general admission ticket, touring companies often ended their runs in more modest local establishments in the so-called "barrios pobres." Houses like San Antonio's Teatro Nacional were at the disposition of the community for national celebrations, community-wide fund raisers, or any other special cultural event. The professional companies also felt responsible for their community as a whole in the United States as well as in Latin America, often donating percentages of the proceeds to establish a clinic or a school in San Antonio, Detroit, New York, or wherever a community was struggling to organize its own life and institutions. Theatres also crusaded to raise funds for flood and earthquake victims in Latin America and for defense committees of unfortunates like Aurelio Pompa, who were being prosecuted by Anglo-American law. The community in turn showed its appreciation for the individual theatrical artists by showering them with gifts during the special benefit performances in their name.

The Great Depression and the forced and voluntary repatriation of Mexicans not only de-populated the communities, but to a great extent also the theatres. In order to survive for a while in the 1930s the theatrical artists banded together in such cooperatives as the Compañía de Artistas Unidos and the Compañía Cooperativa in a valiant effort to buy or rent theatres, manage themselves and eke out a living. But the economy and the commercial interests of theatre owners, who could maximize their own profits by renting films instead of supporting a whole cast, could not sustain their efforts. Those who did not return to Mexico often continued to pursue their art by organizing non-commercial companies that performed to raise funds for community projects and charities. The stage of artists like Daniel Ferreiro Rea in Los Angeles and Carlos Villalongín in San Antonio was amateurish only in the respect that the artists were not paid. They continued to perform many of the same secular dramas, *zarzuelas*, and *revistas* as before. Through their efforts theatre arts were sustained from the 1930s to the 1950s on a voluntary and community basis. A few of the vaudeville performers, like La Chata Noloesca, were able to prolong their professional careers abroad and in New York where Spanish-language vaudeville survived until the sixties. Others like Leonardo García Astol, followed up their vaudeville careers by working in local, Spanish-language radio and television broadcasting after World War II. The tenacious tent theatres also continued their perennial odysseys into the fifties, often setting up right in the camps of migrant farm laborers to perform their *revistas*. It is these traveling theatres that were in part responsible for giving a first exposure of the Hispanic theatrical tradition to some of the young people that would create a Chicano theatre in the late sixties.

Carmen Zapata portrays Isabel la Católica in Bilingual Foundation's and KCET-TV's "Moments to be Remembered."

During the 1950s and 1960s, serious drama was occasionally produced by professionals like Carolina Villalongín and Lalo Astol in San Antonio and on a more regular basis in Los Angeles by playwright Rafael Trujillo Herrera, who constructed and administered his own Teatro Intimo, which is still functioning today.

In the 1970s professional companies began to make a comeback under the leadership of such producers as Hollywood star, Carmen Zapata. Her efforts at the Bilingual Foundation of the Arts, like those of El Teatro de El Paso under Carlos Ayub and Albuquerque's La Compañía under José Rodríguez, are largely supported by local, state and federal arts agencies. These companies, for the most part, produce masterworks by Latin Americans and Spaniards, and occasionally plays by Chicano playwrights like Carlos Morton and Estella Portillo.

But the real theatrical story of the late sixties and the decade of the seventies is the emergence and growth of a dynamic theatrical movement among the youth: Chicano theatre. Born in 1965 under the direc-

A scene from the Los Angeles production of *Zoot Suit*.

tion of Luis Valdez in an effort to assist in organizing farmworkers for the grape boycott and strike, Chicano theatres soon spread to campuses and communities throughout the Southwest. From the very beginning, the hundreds of Chicano theatre groups performed in streets, parks, churches or any space available in order to communicate to the grass roots their social and political messages. From the Chicano theatre movement have sprung many of today's Mexican American actors, directors, filmmakers and drama professors, as well as the first Mexican American play, *Zoot Suit*, to reach Broadway and to become a Hollywood, feature-length film.

With the continued success of the Bilingual Arts Foundation, TENAZ (the national organization of Chicano theatres), El Teatro Campesino in Hollywood, traveling companies like Santa Barbara's El Teatro de la Esperanza and Tucson's Liberatad, Hispanic theatre in the Southwest promises to grow and flourish once again.

BIBLIOGRAPHY

John W. Brokaw, "A Mexican-American Acting Company, 1849-1939," *Educational Theatre Journal* 27/1 (March, 1975), 23-29.

Rosemary Gipson, "The Beginning of Theatre in Sonora," *Arizona and the West* 9/4 (Winter, 1967), 349-364.

Jorge Huerta, *Chicano Theatre: Themes and Forms*. Ypsilanti: Bilingual Review Press, 1982.

Winifred Johnson, "Early Theatre in the Spanish Borderlands," *Mid-America* 13 (October, 1930), 121-131.

Nicolás Kanellos, "Chicano Theatre in the Seventies," *Theatre* 12/1 (Fall, 1980), 33-37.

Nicolás Kanellos, "El teatro profesional hispánico: orígenes en el sudoeste," *La Palabra* 2/1 (Primavera, 1980), 16-24.

Nicolás Kanellos, "The Flourishing of Hispanic Theatre in the Southwest," *Latin American Theatre Review* 16/1 (Fall, 1982).

PHOTO CREDITS

Bancroft Collection, UC-Berkeley, *9, 15*
Bilingual Foundation for the Arts *16*
Francisco Blasco *8*
Caracol Magazine *12*
Leonardo García Astol *13*
William Lansford *10*
Mark Taper Forum *17*
San Antonio Conservation Society *1, 11*
Southwest Museum *5*

ACKNOWLEDGEMENTS

We would like to express our appreciation to the following libraries and special collections that have rescued Mexican American materials and made them accessible to us:

Bancroft Collection, University of California—Berkeley
Benson Latin American Collection, University of Texas at Austin
Chicano Studies Library, University of California—Los Angeles
Chicano Studies Library, University of California—Berkeley
Houston Metropolitan Archives, Houston Public Library
Mexican American Studies Project, Benson Latin American Library, University of Texas at Austin
San Antonio Conservation Society
Southwest Museum, Los Angeles

The following individuals and organizations provided materials, support, and expertise:

Leonardo García Astol, Susie Mijares Astol, Bonnie Britt, Francis Thomas Burke III, Belia Areu Camargo, Richard Chabrán, Elvira Chavarría, Carmen Cubas, Cultural Arts Council of Houston, Barclay Goldsmith, Hispanic International University, The Departments of Spanish and Mexican American Studies of the University of Houston, Galindo Real Estate (San Antonio), Francisco García, Cindy Garza, Soledad Godínez, Lupita Fernández, Jorge Huerta, Institute of Hispanic Culture of Houston, Thomas Kreneck, William Lansford, Librería Española (San Antonio), Natalia López, Nancy Marino, Lydia Mendoza, Rodolfo Mendoza, Bernadette Corrigan Monda, Munguía Printers (San Antonio), Julián Olivares, Narciso Peña, Estella Portillo, Joan Quarm, Idsonil Rivera, Arturo Rosales and the Association of Southwest Humanities Councils, Consuelo Chavez, Leila Smith, George Strimbu, Thomas Strimbu, El Teatro Campesino, Tejano Artists, Inc., Rafael Trujillo Herrera, La Voz de Houston (newspaper), Carolina Villalongín, Tomás Ybarra-Frausto, Romulus Zamora, Carmen Zapata.

Tomás Ybarra-Frausto
Stanford University

La Chata Noloesca:
Figura Del Donaire

Guadalupe Street traverses many of the established barrios on the west side of San Antonio. It is the street one travels to arrive at the venerable San Fernando Cemetery. There amidst the *lápidas* and *bóvedas* one encounters a simple grave marked by a tombstone with the following epitaph:

> Beatriz Noloesca—La Chata
> Artista sanantoniana que con
> su arte hizo sonreír al mundo.
> En Paz descanse

The woman inspiring this eulogy, "La Chata Noloesca," was one of the oustanding comic actresses of Spanish-speaking vaudeville. Beloved by domestic and international audiences during a distinguished theatrical career spanning more than half a century, "La Chata Noloesca" is a significant figure in the history of Spanish-speaking popular theatre in the United States. She was an effervescent comedienne in the bawdy Rabelaisian tradition of the Mexican *farándula carpa*. Hers was a truly popular art arising from and closely aligned to the dreams, hopes and aspirations of the working-class masses who constituted the largest segment of her public throughout the Southwest.

La Chata Noloesca was born Beatriz Escalona on August 20, 1903, in a small house on Medina Street near the Missouri Pacific railroad depot in San Antonio.[1] Her father died while Beatriz was quite young and, to make ends meet, her widowed mother established a thriving business providing hot food for train passengers passing through the city. Intermingling with this diverse clientele served as Beatriz' first encounter with the public.

The *mexicano* community in turn-of-the-century San Antonio maintained a rich and rooted tradition of popular theatre both religious and secular. Collective enactments of the *matachines, posadas, pastorelas* and Easter pageants were as integral a part of daily life as the secular entertainments of the *circos, carpas* and *maromas*. Such expressive

41

forms, understood as both celebration and performance, bonded the spectators and spectacles in a nexus of social interaction. Presentational events undoubtedly contributed to the cohesion of the Mexican-American community, strengthening its cultural identity and providing a sense of security against the alien and encroaching hegemony of the American way of life.

Amidst the hustle and bustle of the rapidly growing city, these entertainments were an occasional treat for the young Beatriz Escalona. However, the more formal conventions of traditional theatre began to strike responsive chords in the imagination of the carefree and impetuous young child. Theatrical yearnings were first stimulated in Mexico. The San Antonio branch of the Escalona family maintained cordial and close contacts with relatives in Monterrey, Mexico. It was customary to travel frequently between the two cities, the usual pattern being that the young Beatriz made extended seasonal visits to her relations who lived near the Teatro Independencia.

That grandiose coliseum, relic of a more opulent epoch, served as a provincial base for traveling companies from the interior of Mexico. In its cavernous and ornate interior, the young *tejanita* sat entranced through programs of serious drama, melodrama, *zarzuela*, and *revista*. Beatriz Escalona developed such an abiding passion for the stage that when funds were not available for admission, she created small bouquets of domestic flowers from her relatives' garden, selling them in order to buy the cheapest seats in the *galería*.

Back home in San Antonio, the Teatro Zaragoza had been established in 1912. In tandem with examples of the nascent Hollywood movie industry, the Zaragoza presented regular seasons of "comedia, drama y variedad." Such stellar attractions as Juan B. Padilla, Concepción Guerrero, Adela and Xochil Hidalgo and Lupe Rivas Cacho performed to sold-out houses. Of all the performers, it was the *tiples*, the specialized singers of *zarzuela* musical airs, who captured the fancy of the young Beatriz Escalona. One can imagine her stage-struck reveries, in which she imagined herself joyously singing and dancing with wild abandon before an adoring public.

Such youthful dreams of stardom were punctured by the reality of having to obtain employment in order to aid her widowed mother in providing for the family. At the age of fifteen, Beatriz became an *acomodadora*, an usherette at the old Teatro Nacional situated on Calle Comercio in the heart of the downtown section of San Antonio that catered to the Mexican population.

Operated by Tano Luccesse, El Nacional later became one of the premiere temples of Spanish-speaking *variedades*. Its inaugural season of 1917 featured the Compañía de María del Carmen Martínez and subsequently many of the great artists of the Spanish-speaking theatre trod its boards.

Recollections of this elegant showcase of the dramatic arts were passed down through oral tradition from Beatriz Escalona to her daughter Belia Camargo, who retrospectively remembers:

> . . . El antiguo Teatro Nacional era lindísimo, con palcos . . . muy espacioso todo . . . acojinados de terciopelo los asientos . . . cosas doradas, muy elegante. Los palcos los vendían a familias por año. En esos tiempos había varios ricachones de aquí de San Antonio que tenían sus palcos y ésos no los tocaba nadie. Cuando venían compañías grandes, ya las familias adineradas tenían su palco. Y para el público general era todo luneta numerada . . .

Ensconced in their deeply cushioned velvet seats, the various segments of the Mexican-American community patronized extended theatrical seasons of operetta, *zarzuela*, *revistas* and *variedades*. If the dominant mood emanating from the stage was one of lightness, gaiety and frivolity, the historical events unraveling outside of the theatre proclaimed an epoch of turbulence and upheaval for Mexicans on both sides of the Texas-Mexican border. The Mexican Revolution (1910-20) was tumultuously transforming Mexican society.

Mexican-American enclaves in Los Angeles, Chicago, El Paso, San Antonio and many other communities integrated thousands of refugees. Among those crossing *al norte* were dramatists, impresarios and theatrical families who brought with them specific performance techniques as well as acting and staging traditions. While these newcomers expanded the customary theatrical experiences of the settled residents, they also brought with them certain attitudes that became pivotal in the subsequent development of popular theatre in the Southwest. The noted folklorist Américo Paredes succinctly defines the prevailing attitudinal range:

> During this period the "Mexiquitos" in the larger cities of the Southwest exhibited two contrasting states of mind. One was a truly refugee state of mind, cultivated especially by the middle-class Mexican but adopted by all older Mexicans, according to which the Mexican's life in the United States was to be insulated from Anglo influences and activities and devoted to the dream of returning to Mexico. Another state of mind was found among the younger people in the barrios, who were being forced to adapt to the environment of Anglo cities and who found acculturation an inevitable product of their fight for survival.[2]

Echoes of these distinct attitudes will remain in the development of Mexican-American *teatro*. The refugee mentality will persist in maintaining affiliation and theatrical reproduction of Mexican popular types, folklore and language. Newly arrived *mexicanos* will applaud *teatro* groups who maintain stock characters and situations: barrio dialogues, *huarache troubadours, pulquería* drunkards, romantic *charros*, downtrodden *inditos* and urban dandies all affirming "this is who we are and this is how we speak!"

At the same time, cultural adaptation also occurs and Mexican-American theatre will incorporate elements from Anglo-American vaudeville and burlesque. The "pocho" emerges as a stock characterization delineated by the wondrous capacity to code switch in Spanish and English. The bicultural, bilingual reality of life in the United States will be most effectively evoked in the *tandas de variedad* where a bill might include a comic sketch spoken in Spanish alternating with a song stylist singing in English.

By 1921, *tandas de variedad* alternating with Hollywood movies (3 shows a day, 4 on weekends) were the staple fare at the Teatro Nacional where Beatriz Escalona was still working as an usherette and in the box office. The Hermanos Areu (a trio of singers and actors) and local San Antonio artist Adela Hidalgo were the seasonal "headliners." Beatriz, with her irrepressible congeniality, had made friends with most of the local and visiting actors. Her beauty, energy and vivacity charmed one of the Areu brothers, who fell in love with her, married her and took her away as part of his troupe.

Under the tutelage of the Areus, distinguished Hispano-American troupers, Beatriz Escalona was trained in their inherited theatrical traditions. Her name was inverted from Escalona to the more theatrical Noloesca, and because of her pert, upturned nose, she was affectionately dubbed "La Chata"; thus was born her stage name of "La Chata Noloesca." Traveling within the *circuito Grenet*, one of the important entertainment circuits of the period, "La Chata" honed her natural comic talents in the highly charged, participatory context of performances before working-class audiences. Response to her routines might be contagious approval or boisterous disapproval but never indifference. As her troupe traversed northern Mexico and the Southwestern United States, "La Chata Noloesca" was slowly forging a personal acting style and honing her verbal routines.

A decisive event in her evolution as a comedienne occurred in the mid-1920s when she worked with the renowned Spanish *tiple*, Dorita Ceprano, a reigning beauty of the period. La Ceprano, recently arrived in Mexico from Europe, was creating a sensation with her performances and a fabulous wardrobe which featured a copy of Josephine Baker's notorious costume consisting solely of a little string of bananas. The same daring and outré routines with which the American Negro entertainer had scandalized Paris were presented by Dorita Ceprano in San Antonio in late evening shows, *sólo para adultos*.

To "La Chata," Dorita Ceprano exemplified the grace, beauty and charm of the vaudevillian *vedette*. La Ceprano was a total presence who could capture and hold an audience with her disarming grace and sense of style. Often appearing on the same bill with Ceprano, "La Chata" came to realize that she possessed an incredible, natural comic sensibility, a *vis cómica*, a face and personality that elicited mirth with her mere appearance on the stage. Every little piece of her stage business was celebrated with ripples of laughter. Slowly Beatriz Noloesca was evolving her characterization of "La Chata" as a quick-witted, playfully mischievous scamp.

The theatrical characterization of the "pelado," later exemplified by Cantinflas as an urban roustabout who lives by his wits, is a staple component of Mexican popular drama. The feminine counterpart, *la peladita*, also derives from a venerable popular tradition starting with the appearance of Emilia Trujillo circa 1910. As Armando de María y Campos has pointed out,

> Emilia Trujillo fue la primera gran tiple mexicana que creó tipos nuestros. Garrida, esbelta, bonita, de belleza típicamente mexicana, cantaba con una voz que era una campanita de plata, y actuando derrochaba gracia y picardía; ella le dio realce a nuestras chinas, a nuestras "peladitas," a nuestras indias, y su "borrachita," ha servido de modelo, a través de los tiempos para que otras artistas con más suerte que Emilia, cimentaran su fama y su fortuna.[3]

La Trujis, deservedly famous as the originator of Mexican national types, was succeeded by such renowned *tiples cómicas* as Lupe Rivas Cacho and Delia Magaña. Together these comediennes delineated the contours of *la peladita* (the marginal lower-class, streetwise woman of the metropolis). Her "figuration" was actualized on the stage from within a lusty comic and linguistic tradition.

The precursors of the peladita type were: Lupe Inclán, famous for her impersonation of drunken hags; Amelia Wilhelmy who presented the aggressive stance and behavior of women in the urban *barriadas* and *vecindades*; together with La Flaca Villegas and La Fufurufa, noted for verbal virtuosity and their use of risqué double entendres. From them all, "La Chata" appropriated elements to forge a distinctly feminine comic style. She also foregrounded language, compressing puns and double meanings into witty stratagems of disarmament. Her characterization of *la peladita*, however, is much lighter than that of her predecessors with an overlay of sweetness and grace. Spontaneous speech play serves as a defining characteristic. "La Chata's" *peladita* speaks to the urban mass with the strengths and flavors of its living language which in itself surfaces as a creative response to conflicting tensions triggered by conflicting cultural loyalties.

By the late 1920s, after prolonged gestation, the theatrical persona of "La Chata Noloesca" strutted into the *tandas de variedad* as a rounded, complex characterization. "La Chata" pranced on stage wearing a ruffled print dress, oxford shoes with gaudy rolled-down socks, her hair parted at the center and combed into a pair of tight *chongos* over the ears. Two saucy *moños* of colored ribbon accented her vivacity. Wide-open expectant eyes emphasized by false eyelashes were a dominant feature of her makeup. The overall impression was of a pert, clever, yet vulnerable maiden.

Schooled in the declamatory, rhetorical and histrionic style of the Mexican emoting tradition, "La Chata Noloesca" developed characterizations with broad strokes and expressive open gestures. Drawing heavily from clowning and miming techniques, the core of her comedy routines was centered on the physicalization of ideas, so that psychological and emotional stages were made externally transparent through physical action. Few words in the routines were left without gestural accompaniment, either facially or bodily. Movement was constant, fast-paced and slapstick. Embedded in every gesture (a scratch, a wink, a smirk) was a piece of stage business aiming for a laugh.

Laughter stimulated by verbal virtuosity is a staple of Mexican comedy. Directly linked to the *picardía* of spoken language, especially among the urban working classes, much humor stems from adroit manipulation of linguistic resources such as puns and double entendres. The *albur,* an aggressive chain of wisecracks predominantly of a sexual nature, is a common source of much proletarian Mexican humor.

Marginalized sectors within the Mexican and Mexican-American subcultures weave pyrotechnical displays of language that often function as subversive strategies against imposed orders and hierarchies. Official political rhetoric, for example, when lampooned by exaggeration, can be rendered ineffectual as soon as its meaningless sloganeering base is exposed.

Tandas de variedad employed many comedy routines involving a *peladito* usually ensnared by authority. As a defense mechanism, the *pelado* directs a torrent of verbiage against his oppressor. Spontaneously composed with verve and crackling wit, such clusters of meaningless banter are not only delightfully amusing, but by their very redundancy they expose the accomplice nature of language to authority. The theatrical example par excellence of such verbal strategies is the inimitable Cantinflas. His dizzyingly convoluted dialogue composed of meaningless vocabulary is humorous because it underscores the vulnerable and fragile nature of human communication codes.

If the form of the Mexican *sentido de humor* is one of conventionalized verbal jousting, its content is well defined by the great comic actor Roberto Soto:

> El público de teatro frívolo en México es muy especial. No se conforma,

para reír, con el chiste natural, esto es, el que sólo lleva gracia. Necesita, para reírlo, que el chiste lleve un contenido político o bien ser de doble sentido. Un chiste político es una característica de la comicidad nuestra.[4]

While political humor defines Mexican comedy, it played a lesser role in Mexican-American *teatro*. Comedy routines might be situationally political (e.g., a meeting between a Mexican worker and the Border Patrol), but dramatically, the humor stemmed from dialogue underscoring verbal play and innuendo.

Making use of many such comic devices and traditions, "La Chata" built comedy routines around a theatrical characterization as a "naughty child." Because of her childlike demeanor, audiences granted her license to create havoc. The public responded indulgently, laughing at her in the same way they would at the *ocurrencias* of a child saying hurtful, if truthful, words. The "naughty child" persona served "La Chata" as a distancing device. Situated at the center of the dramatic action, she nonetheless remained the comic outsider.

It is within the restrictive limits of the dramatic sketch that "La Chata's" comic genius reigned. These brief comical scenes have antecedents in the *pasos* of the classical Spanish stage. Basically they are stagings of jokes or anecdotal situations elaborated for their comic potential. In the *tanda* sketch, action is foregrounded over text. Spontaneous ad-libbing and constant improvisations underscore or comment upon the written text itself.

Sketches rarely develop a plot line but rather work out confrontational situations between authority figures and underlings. Reversals in which the underdog becomes the master are common. Reduced to basic components, sketches are fusions of physical acting styles and verbal comedy. Anglo-American burlesque with its picaresque scenarios, rapid physical action and quick blackouts directly influenced the *tanda* sketches in "La Chata's" repertoire.[5] Following are two of her classic sketches:

Si Se Lo Pone, Lo Pasa

(*The action occurs* en la frontera, *the point of entry between Mexico and the United States.*)

Characters: La Migra *and several Mexican types.*

MIGRA: A ver, déjeme ver su pasaporte. . . . ¿A dónde va?
OBRERO: Voy al otro lado, nada más voy de compras.
MIGRA: Bueno, está bien. Pero ya sabe que todo lo que traiga, se lo
    tiene que traer puesto, . . . si no, no lo pasa.
(*Viene otro y lo mismo.*)
MIGRA: Le digo que si compra algo al otro lado, y regresa, lo tiene que

traer puesto, ¡si no, no pasa!
(Lo chistoso claro es que si es mujer trae puesta cosas de hombre, pantalones, . . . camisas, y los hombres llevan puestos vestidos, brassière, etc. Por fin entra el cómico [La Chata o Doroteo o Laura Guerra].)
COMICO: *(Entra con un gran bulto.)*
MIGRA: ¿Qué trae?, a ver, a ver.
COMICO: Pos no, que esto no se lo doy.
MIGRA: Ya le dije, que lo que traiga se lo tiene que traer puesto, . . . si no, no pasa.
COMICO: Pos esto no me lo pongo.
MIGRA: Bueno mire, ¡ya esoy harto! Le digo que si no se lo pone, no lo pasa.
COMICO: Pos mire, que no me lo pongo *(Saca una lavantina de la bolsa).*
(Blackout o telón rápido.)

El Frijolito

(An interior setting with guests at a party; enter a mischievous child.)

NIÑA: Toma, te voy a dar un frijolito, y a ti también un frijolito, etc. . . .
(Los huéspedes platican, dicen chistes, entra la niña.)
NIÑA: Toma, te doy otro frijolito, y para ti otro frijolito, . . . a cada quien su frijolito . . .
(Entra y sale dos o tres veces.)
HUESPED: Bueno ¿y esta niña de dónde agarra tanto frijolito? A ver, niña, ven, acércate, dime ¿de dónde sacas tanto frijolito?
NIÑA: Pos de aquí . . . *(Enseñando una bacinica).* . . . *(Blackout o telón rápido.)*

The comic world of the sketch revolves around what Mikhail Bakhtine calls the lower stratum,[6] humor related to the drama of bodily life (copulation, birth, growth, eating, drinking and defecation). Some sketches bordered on the scatological in terms of themes or language, but always they were amenable to a *público familial*.

In the *tandas de variedad*, it was not unusual to have a Spanish-language sketch, followed by the dancing of the fox-trot or the English rendition of a pop song. Although some sketches experimented with linguistic code switching, most routines were in Spanish. "La Chata Noloesca" always worked in Spanish.

By the 1930s, the *mexicano* community made up nearly 40 percent of the population of San Antonio. The class structure included political refugees from Mexico's upper classes, a middle segment of professional, technical and managerial occupations and a vast sector of *trabajadores*. Although the dominant mainstream impulse was toward "Americanization," total hegemony of the English language and the Anglo-American way of life was neutralized by the maintenance of Spanish-language newspapers, radio, bookstores and *teatro* in various forms, from opera and *zarzuelas* to *tandas de variedad*. By the end of the 1930s, "La Chata" realized the dream of starting her own company billed as *Atracciones Noloesca, Variedades Mexicanas*. Under this banner, the newly formed company of 16 members, singers, dancers and comedians, made a triumphant debut at the Teatro Alcázar in La Habana, Cuba, shortly before the outbreak of World War II.

Returning to the United States, "La Chata" visited and performed in Mexico, becoming a witness to the emergence of Mexican mass culture. By 1938, Mexico was operating two powerful radio stations, XEQ and XEW, the Mexican film industry was the largest in Latin America; and many aspects of Mexican culture and folklore had been converted into a cultural industry, a powerful instrument of pacification and control. *Teatro popular,* especially the *carpas* and the *revistas,* continued to present an alternative vision to the commodification of Mexican folk culture and popular art.

In San Antonio, the repercussions of the emerging Mexican cultural industry were varied. At the Teatros Nacional and Zaragoza, Mexican films had replaced the Anglo-American "B" movies and cowboy films. However, the Mexican films presented only officially sanctioned visions of Mexican reality. Screen idols began to supplant live performers as objects of adulation. The masses who had supported *las tandas de variedad* started to transfer their allegiance and began clamoring for the newest screen idols: Pedro Infante, Jorge Negrete, Gloria Marín and many others. These silver-screen stars became the headliners in the *tanda* when they traveled north for personal appearances. Local performers in the *variedades* became second-stringers and many did not survive.

This is the period of World War II when the screen extolled the triumphs of the *Escuadrón 201* (Mexican flying aces), and the *tandes de variedad* included patriotic routines of khaki-clad chorines singing "Me Voy de Soldado Razo." Rousing finales always included the presentation of both the Mexican and the American flags. Comedy routines often featured a Pachuco and included dialogue in beautiful hybrid mixtures of English, Spanish and Pachuco caló. Integral parts of the *tandas* were singers whose lyrics projected the realities of life *de acá de este lado*. Song stylists such as Lydia Mendoza, Chelo Silva, Esperanza Espino and Eva Garza joined "La Chata Noloesca" as true exponents of the Mexican-American sensibility.

By the mid-1940s, "La Chata Noloesca" was experiencing her last great triumphs at the Teatro Hispano in New York. Arriving with a two-week contract, she remained for three months to enthusiastic acclaim. Performing in New York for nine years, "La Chata" worked with many of the stellar names in Spanish-language theatre.

The final demise of *las tandas de variedad* in the late 1940s is poignantly recalled by Belia Camargo, "La Chata's" daughter:

Todo esto fue muriendo, poco a poco. Cuando comenzaron las películas empezaron a quitar las variedades, . . . entonces llegó un momento en que ya no ponían variedades. Y nada más película y película, . . . y quitaron las variedades y se acabó todo el show.

For the irrepressible "Chata," the show continued even though the medium of expression had changed. In the mid-1950s, she worked with a radio-drama group in her beloved San Antonio. Acting in half-hour daily stints on a program entitled "Espuelas de Plata" over radio station KCOR, she continued to satisfy her public. This kind of radio drama, conceived and written by Don Lalito Astol, was an instant hit with radio listeners and achieved wide distribution. Later, with the advent of Spanish-language television, she pioneered in the medium, starring in "Las Tandas de la Chata," televised versions of her *tanda* routines, for several seasons.

On her 72nd birthday in 1975, she was honored with a gala theatrical tribute by the many artists with whom she had worked for close to half a century. As a crowning accolade, the National Association of Actors in Mexico awarded "La Chata Noloesca" a diploma of honor. She is one of the few non-Mexican-born actors so honored.

Foreshadowing the end, one day she told her daughter, "Hija, el día que yo muera, que me velen en el Teatro Nacional. Porque de esas tablas salí y allí quiero que me vayan a ver." No one had the heart to tell her that in the name of progress and urban renewal both the Teatro Nacional and the Zaragoza had been demolished. These twin meccas of the Spanish-language dramatic arts had been reduced to rubble and their historic sites converted into parking lots.

On another occasion, while musing on her life and times, she provided a review and summing up of her career:

Yo viví mi vida bien; yo me puedo morir ya porque ya gocé de mi vida. Di mi vida al teatro, a la gente, al público; hice reír a mucha gente. Me voy muy tranquila.

Death came on April 4, 1979. But "La Chata Noloesca's" fame remains alive in the collective memories and imagination of legions of fans. An internal consistency in "La Chata's" work was the positive accentuation of human foibles. She ridiculed them and made us laugh at ourselves but never with derision. Her comedy was restorative rather than mocking, accepting rather than alienating. The genius of "La Chata Noloesca" was that she made us appreciate the world in its droll aspects, in its cheerful relativity. Through humor, "La Chata Noloesca" reminded us of one of our highest spiritual privileges, the ability to confront adversity with cheer. Through the universal spirit of laughter, she underscored Aristotle's ancient formula: "Of all living creatures, only humans are endowed with laughter."

[1] Biographical material provided by Sra. Belia Areu Camargo in an interview conducted at San Antonio, Texas, December 21, 1981.

[2] Américo Paredes, *A Texas Mexican Cancionero* (Urbana: University of Illinois Press, 1976), p. 153.

[3] Armando María Y Campos, *El Teatro de Género Chico en la Revolución Mexicana* (México: Biblioteca del Instituto Nacional de Estudios Históricos de la Revolución Mexicana, 1956), p. 72.

[4] Quoted in María y Campos, p. 438.

[5] Sra. Belia Areu Camargo commented that some of "La Chata's" sketches were nothing more than translations of Anglo-American burlesque skits embellished with the traditions of Mexican humor.

[6] This carnivalesque spirit is discussed in Mihail Bakhtine's *Rabelais and his World*, Tr. Helene Iswolsky (Cambridge: M.I.T. Press, 1968).

Armando Miguélez
University of Arizona

El Teatro Carmen (1915-1923):
Centro del Arte Escénico Hispano en Tucson

Para hacer una historia completa del teatro hispano en el suroeste de los Estados Unidos necesitamos partir de presupuestos teóricos que transciendan los límites del género "teatro" según se concibe en la historiografía occidental. Los estudios semióticos que se han hecho últimamente nos permiten ampliar las manifestaciones teatrales hasta límites que desde el Renacimiento no era posible.

Tenemos que darnos cuenta que la palabra "teatro" viene del verbo que significa "mirar" y miramos a aquello que nos llama la atención. Por esto, teatro en un sentido amplio, es todo gesto humano hecho para captar la atención de un público que mira hacia ello y se deleita viéndolo. Umberto Eco dice que "el elemento primario de una representación teatral está dado por un cuerpo humano que se ostenta y se mueve."[1] En este sentido, todo espectáculo o diversión pública hecha para el deleite de alguien más, de un público, es una forma teatral. A partir de aquí el teatro ha añadido otros elementos como los verbales, los escenográficos, etc., aunque también, se ha dado el fenómeno opuesto, de ir depurándose hasta llegar a ser sólo un movimiento corporal como en las técnicas escénicas de Jerzy Grotowski.[2]

Entendiendo así el teatro tenemos que ir a las fiestas o celebraciones públicas para encontrar las primeras manifestaciones teatrales en Tucson en el siglo XIX. Las fiestas más importantes en Tucson a principios de siglo eran las religiosas (San Juan, Corpus Cristi, Navidad, Semana Santa), las celebraciones familiares (santos, bautismo, bodas), las fiestas civiles (rodeos, tientas de ganado, carreras de caballos, palenques, etc.), y con el transcurso del tiempo, las fiestas patrióticas (16 de septiembre y 5 de mayo). Todas estas fiestas por todo el suroeste presentan formas parateatrales como desfiles, procesiones, "shows" musicales y bailables, payasos y pantomimas.[3]

Juntamente con estas manifestaciones teatrales, en la segunda mitad del siglo XIX en Tucson comenzaron a desarrollarse también el teatro religioso y el teatro civil. El primero tiene sus manifestaciones en la obras de orientación litúrgica (siguiendo los ciclos litúrgicos del nacimiento y muerte de Cristo) que fueron tradicionales por todo el suroeste.[4] El teatro civil comienza con los romerioramas, que ejecutaban números circenses, de pantomima y mimo.[5] Después comienzan a venir de Sonora compañías de teatro que ponen en Tucson el "dernier cri" de la escena en los principales teatros de la cuidad de México, La Habana y Madrid. Junto con este teatro representado se dio un teatro escrito de corte histórico como la traducción del francés de *Juárez o la guerra de México* que apareció primero en *La República* de San Francisco y después en *El Fronterizo* de Tucson en 1881, antes que la traducción en forma de libro apareciera en México en 1888.

En el siglo XX las compañías ambulantes continuaron viniendo, ahora con más asiduidad, debido a la gran demanda de teatro dramático que la clase media mexicana de Tucson, compuesta de las viejas familias y los nuevos exilados políticos de la Revolución Mexicana, exigía.

El 20 de mayo de 1915 se inauguró el Teatro Carmen de Tucson. Había habido teatros mexicanos antes en la ciudad—El Cervantes y El Principal en el siglo XIX y El Royal y El Clifton en el XX—pero el hecho de la inauguración de un teatro exclusivamente hecho para albergar las compañías que ponían obras en español, parece que conmovió al público si juzgamos por El Cronista (pseudónimo del crítico de teatro del periódico *El Tucsonense):* "Con un gran éxito artístico y pecuniario y como lo anunciaban sus elegantes y de buen gusto programas se verificó el estreno del Teatro Carmen . . ." El Cronista describe después el teatro: "Su palco escénico amplio, brillantemente iluminado, con magníficos y artísticos decorados y con los reputados y siempre aplaudidos artistas con que se inauguró, fue la nota más simpática por su novedad, de arte y sociedad que puede registrar nuestra crónica en la presente semana." Como se ve el reseñista no parece estar en una ciudad típica del oeste, con vaqueros y cafés cantantes. Sus descripciones presentan todo la pretensión de un evento artístico característico, más que de una ciudad fronteriza y provinciana, de un centro artístico de renombre.

Tucson tenía aproximadamente 15.000 habitantes de los que el 50% eran mexicanos con un sector grande de pequeños comerciantes y clase media mexicanos. Este grupo fue el que apoyó el teatro profesional mexicano en la ciudad que hizo necesario las edificaciones como el Teatro Carmen que dieran cabida a las compañías ambulantes que tenían en sus repertorios dramas y espectáculos considerados de prestigio por las clases medias e ilustradas. Estos grupos mexicanos querían, con eventos artísticos de "categoría," quitar la imagen de villorrio inculto que Tucson tenía. Este sector apoyó las instituciones educativas como la universidad y promovió el teatro, las óperas y la zarzuela a cuyas funciones invitaba a los "hombres prominentes" de la sociedad angloamericana. La imagen del "viejo pueblo" quedaba atrás. Sólo se recordaba como parte de la historia, una historia que le daba abolengo y que hacía a Tucson semejante a las ciudades misionales de California. Esto era muy importante porque es en esta época cuando el angloamericano descubre la California idílica de las misiones. Los antiguos mexicanos de Tucson recordaban el pueblo con nostalgia: su camaradería, sus árboles frondosos, sus fértiles valles, sus costumbres, sus fiestas, sus bailes, sus viejas instituciones. Sin embargo, a esta conciencia histórica se juntaba la idea decimonónica del progreso material. Se alababa el nuevo Tucson: sus instituciones bancarias, sus comercios, sus edificaciones. Tucson en aquel entonces era la residencia de los dueños de las minas y los ranchos de la zona sur de Arizona. Los mexicanos controlaban los ranchos (agricultura y ganadería) y ciertos sectores del comercio.

En este contexto se construye el Teatro Carmen, localizado en la Calle Meyer (384 S. Meyer), una calle de pequeños comerciantes mexicanos y de mucho movimiento en el Tucson de 1915. El teatro tenía una capacidad de 1.400 personas, el más grande de la ciudad.[6] Tenía su foro o palestra y tres secciones en la cávea: platea, luneta y galería. El solar fue comprado por la familia Vázquez en 1883 a Leopoldo Carrillo. En 1914, Ramón Vázquez lo pasa a su esposa, Carmen Soto de Vázquez. Ella edifica un teatro en el lugar que se inaugura el 20 de mayo de 1915 con la obra *Cerebro y Corazón* de la autora potosina Farias Isassi. Este hecho cambia la vida cultural de Tucson. El Teatro Clifton en este momento, venía poniendo obras dramáticas menores, desde luego nunca llegando al drama. El Royal, de las hermanas Aros, ponía en aquellas fechas, cine. El Elysean Grove y el Opera House ponían de vez en cuando obras mexicanas dramáticas o operísticas pero las alternaban con producciones en inglés. Ahora El Carmen se iba a dedicar exclusivamente a obras escénicas de alta calidad hechas por autores y compositores consagrados de México y el resto de los países hispanoamericanos y lo iba a hacer de una manera regular. Las compañías ambulantes en sus "tours" podían incluir a Tucson porque ya tenían un local donde representar y además con un aforo grande que les podía dejar ganancias. Su dueña, Carmen Soto de Vázquez, es consciente de su papel de promotora cultural y social y pone el teatro a disposición de la gente para que tenga la oportunidad de disfrutar de formas artísticas características de su cultura y para que yendo y apoyando estas funciones se contribuya a la retención cultural en la cuidad.

Las compañías ambulantes que primero se quedaron en el teatro fueron La Nacional, que fue la compañía que lo inauguró, y la Compañía de Opera, Opereta y Zarzuela "Millanés-Caballé." Estas compañías ponían en sus funciones, como era habitual entonces, una obra dramática y alguna pieza corta humorística o musical, por lo que estas compañías en sus repertorios debían tener de todo un poco. Las dos compañías anteriormente citadas terminaron por juntarse y actuar en El Carmen con repertorios mixtos (dramas y musicales) y estuvieron en cartel en El Carmen hasta el 9 de junio de 1915. A partir de entonces Carmen Soto anuncia la presencia en su coliseo de varios actores que se habían descolgado de diferentes compañías que habían llegado a la cuidad: Elena de la Llata, Arturo Carrillo y Raquel Flores de la compañía Arias-Turich-Serazzi y Elena Madrigal de "La Nacional."

Al cabo de un mes de estar funcionando solamente como teatro, pasó también a ser cine. Alternaba el cine con presentaciones en vivo de géneros más ligeros como piezas cantadas y bailadas como las presencias en junio y agosto de 1915 de los cupletistas Higares y Novelty. En agosto del mismo año vuelve al teatro de nuevo el drama, esta vez con *La Dolores*, drama español de Feliú y Codina puesta por la compañía Inclán-Figueroa-Guzmán. La obra es una tragicomedia en la que la pasión dramática volcada en un triángulo amoroso se ve salpicada por las gracias del sargento Rojas. La compañía actuó durante diez días en El Carmen poniendo obras como *Xochitl, Mar y Cielo, El Señor Cura* y *San Juan de Luz*. Sus artistas son volubles y dominan su repertorio a la perfección. Lupita Inclán, la actriz principal, es un claro ejemplo de esto. El crítico de *El Tucsonense* la describe así:

> . . . esa talentosa chiquilla que a diario se nos transforma, caracterizando cuantos tipos se le encomiendan; la virtuosa, la casquivana, la rabiosa, la humilde y por último, la señora pretenciosa, altiva, ampulosa y enfática de 56 años; y lo hermoso es que persuade, que convence y deja de ser La Lupita, para convertirse en Doña Clara de *Las riendas del gobierno* o la Juana de *Más val maña . . ."* (*El Tucsonense*, 25 agosto 1915)

Otras dos compañías escenifican obras en el Carmen en 1915—La Compañía de Zarzuela y Verso "Enrique Moreno"[7] y "La Internacional." El éxito fue grande e incluso los periódicos exhortan a que compren los boletos con anticipación porque a veces la gente tenía que quedar fuera.

En 1916 el Teatro Carmen sólo albergó una compañía de teatro: la compañía "Nacional" con la que se había inaugurado. En los últimos meses del año sirvió de centro político. En él se reunía el Club Neutral, grupo político mexicano que ejerció mucha influencia en las elecciones de ese año. También era el lugar donde se presentaban los candidatos que hacían campaña entre los mexicanos.

En 1917 pasa por El Carmen el cuadro de zarzuela y variedades de los Hermanos Areu, "Sexteto Estrella," que puso, en tres días en marzo, zarzuelas y diferentes bailables. También la compañía de operetas vienesas y drama de gran aparato "Ricardo de la Vega" que se quedó en El Carmen dos semanas en julio de este año, poniendo las operetas clásicas como *La viuda alegre, La casta Suzana* y *Sangre de artista* y dramas como *Juárez y Maximiliano*. El crítico teatral de *El Tucsonense* no sabe qué alabar más, si la buena declamación de la compañía o el hecho de la aceptación de su arte por el público escogido de la ciudad.[8]

En 1918, además del "Novel," que ya había actuado en El Carmen en diciembre de 1917, pasaron por El Carmen la compañía "Angela Méndez," el cuadro "Multicolor," cuadro de variedades y zarzuelas, y la compañía "Virginia Fábregas." El cuadro "Novel" era una compañía de drama, zarzuela y baile que vino a Tucson varias veces, dos de ellas al Carmen a finales de 1917 y en abril-mayo de 1918. El repertorio de esta compañía era muy extenso, unas 100 obras, de las que puso 34 en sus funciones en El Carmen, sin repetir ninguna. La compañía "Angela Méndez" estuvo en la ciudad nueve días escenificando obras senti-mentales como *Amor salvaje* de Echegaray y *La llorona*.

El cuadro "Multicolor" es la primera compañía que trae al Carmen números de magia y prestidigitación. También en sus números de variedades tenía temas de la Revolución como "La Cucaracha."[9] La compañía de la gran actriz mexicana Virginia Fábregas dio cuatro funciones poniendo el drama en cuatro actos *Fedora* de Victoriano Sardou, *El mal que nos hacen* de Jacinto Benavente, *Al amparo de la ley* (probablemente presentado en forma bilingüe a juzgar por el anuncio bilingüe del carte anunciador) y *El genio alegre* de los Hermanos Quintero. Sus presentaciones, aunque anunciadas con gran espectación, no provocaron extensas reseñas en los periódicos como lo hicieron otras presentaciones de otras compañías.

En 1919 la propietaria arrendó el teatro a los Sres. Guzmán y Moreno que volvieron a fomentar la diversificación del teatro. En marzo hay una función de ópera, la compañía de ópera italiana "Graziani-Castillo-Mondragón." A su paso por Tucson en su vuelta a México, la compañía pone en El Carmen la ópera *Lucía de Lammermoor* de Donizetti. A la vez, el teatro pone cine y trae otras distracciones como la compañía de variedades "American Review," los "Perros Comediantes," del Profesor Tenof y los cuadros de variedades "Los More-Rubí," "Los Vencedores," "Bela Oropesa" y "Dueto Rodo-Berty." En mayo acoge a la compañía de drama y zarzuela "María del Carmen Martínez" que cautiva al público sobre todo con su obra *La guerra europea* del director de la compañía Luis G. de Quevedo, que a la vez es autor de otra obra del repertorio, *Pro-patria*. *La guerra europea* llega al fondo de la comunidad exiliada, inmigrada o simplemente nostálgica y ávida de arte de México. *El Tucsonense* la describe así:

> La piececita es en lo general, una filigrana de inspiración, en donde la verdad campea y en donde con matices de vivo colorido se destaca el espíritu de nuestra nacionalidad mexicana. Nuestro pueblo que sabe sentir los borbotones de la sangre azteca al solo recuerdo de la patria o a la sola visión de los colores nacionales, supo premiar a María

Carmen que en gracioso traje nacional representó, en la obra de que nos ocupamos, a México: y la florida verba de nuestro pueblo, puesta en labios de la inteligente artista, nos hizo recordar una y otra vez, nuestro espíritu bravío y nuestra nobleza de abolengo. (29 mayo 1919)

Pro-patria es una zarzuela de Luis G. de Quevedo con música de José Alonzo Pajares. *El Mosquito* lo describe así:

La obrita en cuestión es patriótica por demás y encierra en sí un verdadero espíritu de unificación, especialmente entre el elemento mexicano en este país que se encuentra desunido por cuestión de credos políticos. (15 junio 1919)

A finales de 1919 acuden al Carmen dos compañías de operetas y zarzuelas, la "Arte Nuevo" y la "Mimí-Derba-Caballé." Pero ahora el público que había acogido con tanto interés a todas estas compañías, empieza a fallar. *El Tucsonense* dice de la función de la "Mimí-Derba-Caballé": "Lástima que nuestro públio no sepa concurrir a estas hermosas fiestas de positivo arte y contento" (18 diciembre 1919). El competidor más serio del teatro en este momento no es el cine, sino el boxeo. Está en los "rings" el tucsonense Alberto "Happy" Woods que arrastra las multitudes. En su pelea en el Elysean Grove con Desmarias, atrae a 3.000 espectadores. También surge ahora otro fenómeno nuevo en el ambiente teatral de la ciudad, la de las compañías de aficionados que a veces ponen sus obras gratis o sólo pidiendo donaciones para alguna obra benéfica. La situación del teatro y demás funciones musicales y de variedades es tal que al pasar por aquí el "Dueto Llera" en su gira a El Paso, San Antonio, New Orleans y Philadelphia, Carlos Jácome invita a los miembros prominentes angloamericanos y mexicanonorteamericanos por nombre para que acudan a una función del dueto y así muestren su buen gusto y apreciación hacia el Divino Arte. A. Cota Robles, que ya desde 1918 venía arengando a los tusconenses para que asistieran al teatro,[10] escribe en febrero de 1920 su artículo "¿Es Tucson una ciudad culta?" en la que pone en tela de juicio la sofisticación artística de la ciudad por su falta de interés en la música y el teatro.

En mayo hace su aparición el "Cuadro Iris" y a juzgar por *El Tucsonense*, llenó el teatro. Sin embargo, el teatro cierra y hasta el 11 de diciembre no vuelve a abrir, esta vez bajo el arrendatario Sr. Daniel A. Penedo. La compañía "César Sánchez" viene a los escenarios tucsonenses y los logra animar con su novedad más exitosa, *Santa* (de Federico Gamboa), la telenovela de entonces que estaba haciendo pavor en México y otros países hispanoamericanos. El enredo consiste en que una joven seducida por un militar es descubierta por su madre que logra apartarla de él. Este se va a la guerra a tierras lejanas y la madre, avergonzada de su hija, la aborrece. Ella, despreciada por su familia, se lanza al mundo y va de mal en peor hasta que encuentra la muerte. La obra tuvo mucho éxito del público en Tucson aunque al crítico de *El Tucsonense* parece que no le gustó: ". . . es como todas las obras de ese género, un tanto cuanto movida para el lado de las emociones" (21 diciembre 1920). El motivo por el que la compañía dejó de representar en el Teatro Carmen no está claro, pero el 29 de diciembre del mismo año tiene instalada una carpa en el lado oeste de la ciudad en la que pone dos zarzuelas—*Enseñanza librea* y *Chin-Chun-Chan*. De vuelta a Hermosillo la compañía sigue haciendo teatro de carpa y los teatros locales ponen presión al juzgado del Distrito de Sonora para que embargue la carpa con la excusa de haber sido pasada por aduanas de contrabando. César Sánchez, según el corresponsal de *El Tucsonense* en Hermosillo, alega "que sólo se debe ese lío a que los dueños de teatros, resentidos porque no les paga renta, buscaron la manera de perjudicarle, pues que la carpa referida está usada ya, y perteneciendo a las putiles de la compañía, no se les ha cobrado derecho alguno, no los causa" (*El Tucsonense*, 12 marzo 1921).

En 1921 el teatro otra vez aparece con diferentes propósitos: cine, teatro, salón de baile y "ring" de boxeo. La compañía de teatro con la que comenzó el año fue la de los Hermanos Vendrell, grupo infantil que pone en escena la pieza *El sacristán Ropavelas*. Después pasó a ser un "ring" de boxeo y es entonces cuando la ciudad cerró el teatro como lugar público por no reunir las condiciones de resistencia para un concurso numeroso de público y por carecer de salidas suficientes para que la concurrencia pudiera salir en caso de accidentes. *El Tucsonense* saca la noticia en primera página y publica un editorial al respecto diciendo que es raro que un edificio que se había usado por seis años con todos los requisitos exigidos por la ley, de pronto ya no cumple los requisitos. El periódico cree que su condición no es tan mala como la de otros edificios en el centro de la ciudad y dice que la ley debe ser igual para todos (26 marzo 1921).

El año 1922 es el último en que El Carmen funciona como teatro propiamente, mezclando este propósito con el de tallerescuela y con el de sala de baile. Las dos últimas compañías que vienen al Carmen son la de Teresa Montoya y la de "Espectáculos Modernos." La primera permanece en el teatro seis días poniendo siete funciones (*Magda* de Sudderman, *El Bastardo o Papá Lebonard*, *Adiós juventud*, *La enemiga*, *El herrero de Ohnet*, *La malquerida* de Benavente y *Zazá*). El crítico de *El Tucsonense* le dedica las mejores reseñas escritas en los periódicos en español desde la inauguración del teatro. Dice que esta vez no está hablando con hipérbole, que esta compañía es insuperable, con una característica muy importante—"La homogeneidad en el grupo." Sólo se lamenta que la entrada no hubiera sido mayor. La poca asistencia de público se debió a factores externos: mal tiempo, confusión de fechas en los programas, malas condiciones económicas y enfermedades en la comunidad. Reseñando la actuación de la compañía en la obra *Magda* dice:

> Los aplausos como ondas hertizianas partían de un extremo a otro del salón desde las primeras escenas y en suma, el público salió de allí, del Carmen como saboreando algo que ya hacía mucho tiempo no probaba; el arte diluido en el espíritu gota a gota que ejerce un irresistible influjo y realiza un "masaje" espiritual. *(El Tucsonense,* 1 abril 1922).

La compañía de "Espectáculos Modernos" presentaba de todo un poco—zarzuela, baile, drama, comedia y canto. Debutó en El Carmen el 19 abril 1922 con *Tierra baja* de Guimerá y la zarzuela *El pobre Valbuena* y se despidió del público de Tucson el 7 de mayo con zarzuelas *(La gatita* y *Ya somos tres)* y variedades. La compañía, a pesar de su buena presentación, no logró suficiente concurrencia y El Carmen deja de usarse como teatro para pasar a ser una sala de baile primero y después un "ring" de boxeo.

En 1926 Carmen Soto lo traspasa a Elena Cervantes. En 1927 el edificio era un garaje. Por entonces de los tres teatros con presentaciones regulares en español en 1915, sólo quedaba uno, El Royal, que desapareció en los 30 con el decaimiento general del teatro en la ciudad con motivo de la depresión económica y el auge del cine hablado.

El teatro de taquilla en español había muerto en Tucson. En los 30 comienzan a tener más éxito las compañías de aficionados de la ciudad, afiliados a grupos o clubs religiosos, cívicos o culturales. Estos grupos continuaron poniendo el mismo tipo de obra que el que ponían las compañías ambulantes si bien ya fueron incorporando más creaciones locales.[11]

El teatro, presentado en estos teatros, aunque en cierto sentido colonizado por el teatro producido y creado fuera de las fronteras de los Estados Unidos, cumplía una función cultural muy importante. El teatro, las actividades eclesiásticas y la familia fueron los núcleos que mantuvieron viva y sin interrupciones la vena cultural por toda la primera mitad del siglo XX. Además, la participación de la gente en estos eventos creó una especie de comunión de gustos que hizo posible la legación y el remozamiento cultural. Como muy bien ha dicho Nicolás Kanellos: "The professional theatre houses became the temples of culture where the Mexican Hispanic community as a whole could gather."[12] Los críticos, cuando arengaban a que el público fuera al teatro, no sólo valoraban los valores intrínsecos de la obra sino también su grado de mexicanidad. Las críticas a las obras de temas alejados eran más de tipo estético o de belleza en la actuación de los actores; cuando la obra presentaba algo que tocaba la cuerda de la sensibilidad nacionalista, entonces se resaltaba el contenido. Cuando la compañía "Ricardo de la Vega" puso el drama *Juárez y Maximiliano,* el crítico hace esta recensión:

> La interpretación fue correcta y el público, patriota, leal y verdaderamente sentimental, se electrizó a la sola presencia del hermoso pabellón de Igual, cuando en las manos heroicas del valiente Coronel Rosas, flameó el soplo de la Gloria y el Triunfo.
>
> Mucho, mucho agradó la representación de la obra puesta en escena el lunes último y hubo quien asistió a ella sólo por el placer de ver cómo caían los traidores, tal vez con intención de poderlos clasificar a la hora de las reivindicaciones. (*El Tucsonense*, 18 julio 1917)

El Teatro Carmen, como los muchos teatros por todo el suroeste de los Estados Unidos, ofreció la oportunidad de que aparecieran en la escena artistas mexicanos que presentaban personajes positivos de la cultura hispano-mexicana. La gente en las colonias mexicanas estaba harta de los estereotipos mexicanos presentados en el cine angloamericano de la época.[13] Este teatro presentaba la otra cara de la moneda y por eso no era apreciado sólo por su valor estético, sino que cumplía otra labor, la de servir de afianzamiento de una cultura, valores y lengua, constantemente denigrados por la mayoría. *El Cosmopolita* de Kansas City en 1919, saliendo al paso de las declaraciones pro-asimilacionistas del gobierno norteamericano, dice: "¿Cómo ser ciudadanos de un país cuya prensa publica todos los días falsedades e injustas opiniones acerca de nuestra querida patria, cuyos artistas sólo se exhiben en películas y cartelones como bandidos y degenerados? ¿Cómo ser conciudadanos de quienes apenas oyen decir 'Mexican' y cierran sus puertas y esconden sus vírgenes?"[14]

En este sentido sociológico las obras teatrales, aunque la mayoría de ellas no tenían una referencia concreta a la situación social inmediata, cumplieron con la función de resistir y de nuetralizar en el grupo la discriminación y etnocentrismo reinantes.

[1] Umberto Eco, "Elementos preteatrales de una semiótica del teatro" en *Semiología del teatro*, Barcelona: Planeta, 1975, p. 96.

[2] Jerzy Grotowski, *Hacia un teatro probre*, México, D. F.: Siglo XXI, 1970.

[3] Podemos ver esta teatralidad en la descripción que hace *Las Dos Repúblicas* de Tucson (9 de septiembre de 1877) de una procesión en honor de San Agustín, fiesta patronal de Tucson: "Pero cuando pudo notarse en toda su plenitud y con más ostentación desarrollado el celo cristiano y amor profundo que anima a las almas hacia su patrón, fue en la noche del martes, en la procesión que salió alrededor de la plaza. Todos los edificios que circundan la misma se hallaban profundamente iluminados en farolitos de colores, brillantes luces de Bengala se cruzaban en el espacio dejando preciosas y refulgentes estelas de variadísimos tintes y en medio de esta bellísima escena destacábase majestuosa, imponente la procesión que con mayor orden marchaba guiada por una inmensa hilera doble de lo más selecto de nuestra sociedad que ataviados lujosamente y con luces innumerables presidiendo al Santo Patrón presentaban un espléndido espectáculo tras el mismo caminaba también un inmenso concurso que literalmente ocupaba toda la extensión de la plaza." En el programa de las fiestas patrias de San Bernardino, California, leemos: "Partirá del Anfiteatro el convite de toros, precedido por su Payaso y Pantomimas, el cual recorrerá las principales calles al son de la Banda Mexicana . . ." (*El Fronterizo*, Tucson,

7 septiembre 1895).

[4] John E. Englekirk, "Notes on the Repertoire of the New Mexican Folk Theatre" en *Southern Folklore Quarterly* 4/4 (Dec. 1940), pp. 227-237.

[5] En John Lockwood "The Life of the Old Pueblo," Atanasia Santa Cruz le cuenta al autor de este tipo de teatro en el decenio de 1850. Hilario Gallego también recuerda estas compañías de saltimbanquis que los solían divertir en la dura vida del presidio de Tucson en los 50. "Reminiscences of an Arizona Pioneer" in *Arizona Historical Review* 6 (Jan. 1935), p. 78.

[6] Había en mayo de 1915 cinco teatros en Tucson: Elysean Grove, the Opera House, The Royal, The Clifton y El Carmen. Tres de ellos ponían obras en español, uno cine y otro obras en inglés.

[7] Esta compañía se juntó con los cupletistas Higares-Novelty y pusieron en el Royal (Oct. 1915) un amplio repertorio de formas teatrales como canto, bailes, monólogos, diálogos, cuplés, murgas, comedias y sainetes.

[8] Dice *El Tucsonense:* "Incuestionablemente Tucson ha estado de gala durante la última semana, aseveración que queda plenamente demostrada con el muy significativo hecho de que el Teatro Carmen ha sido noche a noche regiamente engalanado con las bellezas de esta simpática población que ávidas de las delicias primorosas del divino arte y de una correcta y clásica declamación no han querido perder la rara oportunidad de escuchar las hermosísimas operetas vienesas y dramas de gran aparato que la empresa "Ricardo de la Vega" ha estado poniendo en escena" (18 julio 1917).

[9] El anunciador en *El Tucsonense* exhorta a la compañía para que canten de esta canción la version que dice "Con las barbas de . . ." (5 octubre 1918).

[10] A. Cota Robles, "Aliento" en *El Tucsonense*, 18 mayo 1918, p. 4, col. 2.

[11] Se escenficaron alegorías, revistas y sainetes de ambiente local como *Tucson en camisa*, *Five cents la copia*, *Revista de los pachucos*, *La gloria de la Raza*, y *La bandera de la Alianza*.

[12] Nicolás Kanellos, "The Flourishing of Hispanic Theatre in the Southwest," por aparecer en *Latin American Theatre Review*, 16/1 (Fall, 1982).

[13] Allen Woll, *Latin Image in American Film*, Los Angeles: UCLA, Latin American Center Publications, 1977.

[14] "Sobre Americanización" en *El Cosmopolita*, 11 octubre 1919 (reproducido en *El Mosquito*, Tucson, 25 octubre 1919, p. 2).

FUNCIONES EN EL TEATRO CARMEN

C = Compañía

O = Obra

F = Fecha

N = Nota

C: La Nacional
O: Cerebro y Corazón (Drama de Teresa Farias de Isassi), 20 mayo 1915
    La Señora Capitana (zarzuela), 20 mayo 1915
    La Mandiga, 23 mayo 1915
    María Antonieta (drama histórico), 25 mayo 1915
N: *El Tucsonense,* 12, 22, 26 mayo 1915, p. 4, col. 3

C: Millanés-Caballé y La Nacional
O: Papá Martín (drama), 27 mayo 1915
    Chin-Chun-Chan (zarzuela), 27 mayo 1915
    Chateaux-Margaux (zarzuela), 29 mayo 1915
    Amar sin dejarse amar (sainete), 29 mayo 1915
    El Puñao de Rosas (género chico), 29 mayo 1915

El anillo de hierro, 30 mayo 1915
Juárez y Maximiliano (drama), 31 mayo 1915
El bueno de Guzmán y Chin-Chun-Chan, 1 junio 1915
Los molinos cantan (opereta holandés), 3 junio 1915
Chucho el roto (drama en 6 actos), 4 junio 1915
Molinos que cantan, 5 junio 1915
El encanto de un vals (opereta), 6 junio 1915 y 8 junio 1915
Musas latinas y Marcha de Cádiz (zarzuelas), 9 junio 1915

N: El Tucsonense, 26, 30 mayo 1915; 2, 5, 9 junio 1915

C: Higares y Novelty (cupletistas)
F: 27 junio 1915, 8 agosto 1915
N: El Tucsonense, 26 junio, 7 agosto 1915

C: Inclán-Figueroa-Guzmán
O: La Dolores (de Feliu y Codina, drama español)
F: 17 agosto 1915
N: El Tucsonense, 14, 18 agosto 1915

O: Xochitl
F: 21 agosto 1915
N: El Tucsonense, 21, 25 agosto 1915

C: Inclán
O: El Sr. Cura (comedia en 2 actos)
San Juan de la Luz (zarzuela)
F: 28 agosto 1915
N: El Tucsonense, 28 agosto 1915

C: F. Aguilar
O: La fiesta de San Antón (zarzuela), 4 sept. 1915
La bella Lucerito (zarzuela), 4 sept. 1915
Chin-Chun-Chan (zarzuela de costumbres mexicanas), 5 sept. 1915
Basta de suegros, 5 sept. 1915
N: El Tucsonense, 4, 9 sept. 1915

C: Compañía de Enrique Moreno
O: Un ángel más en el cielo o el médico de los pobres (de Joaquín Santero, drama
social en tres actos)
F: 2 octubre 1915
N: El Tucsonense, 2 octubre 1915

C: Enrique Moreno
O: El hombre es débil (zarzuela)
Cierre usted su puerta (comedia)
Por una mala lengua (comedia)
F: 7 octubre 1915
N: El Tucsonense, 5, 9 octubre 1915

C: Enrique Moreno
O: Los descamisados (zarzuela)
Toros de punta (zarzuela)
Entre dos fuegos (comedia)

F: 10 octubre 1915
N: *El Tucsonense*, 9 octubre 1915

C: Internacional
O: Los Granujas (zarzuela)
La L. L. (zarzuela)
El terrible pez (zarzuela)
F: 13 octubre 1915
N: *El Tucsonense*, 13 octubre 1915

O: Pastorela de José Castelán
F: 22 diciembre 1915
N: *El Tucsonense*, 22 diciembre 1915

C: La Nacional
O: Los plebeyos (drama moderno)
La niña de los besos
F: 12 febrero 1916
N: *El Tucsonense*, 5 febrero 1916

C: La Nacional
O: La malquerida
El místico
La Abadía de Castro
Hidalgo o el grito de Dolores
El compañero de San Pablo
Locura de amor
Los tres mosqueteros
La mujer adúltera
El hijo pródigo
F: Durante la temporada de 1916 a partir del 12 de febrero

C: Quinteto Bohemio
F: 22 abril 1916
N: *El Tucsonense*, 22 abril 1916

C: Aficionados del Teatro Carmen
O: El mundo al revés o la isla de San Balandrán
F: 17 febrero 1917

C: Sexteto Estrella de los Hermanos Areu (compañía de zarzuela, variedad)
O: El hijo del Coronel
F: 4 marzo 1917
N: *El Tucsonense*, 7 marzo 1917

C: "Ricardo de la Vega" (compañía de operetas vienesas y drama de gran aparato)
O: La viuda alegre, 6 julio 1917
La princesa del dólar, 7 julio 1917
La casta Suzana, 8 julio 1917
Las musas latinas, 9 julio 1917
El país de los cartones, 9 julio 1917
La fornarina o la Virgen de Rafael, 10 julio 1917
Sangre de artistas, 11 julio 1917

El soldado de chocolate, 13 julio 1917
Molinos cantan, 14 julio 1917
Eva, 15 julio 1917
La cuarta plana
Chin-Chun-Chan (de Rafael Medina), 15 julio 1917
Los lloridos Juárez y Maximiliano, 16 julio 1917
La viuda alegre, 18 julio 1917
El encanto de un vals, 17 julio 1917
El Conde de Luxemburgo, 19 julio 1917
Las mujeres vienesas, 20 julio 1917
N: *El Tucsonense*, 11, 14, 18 julio 1917

C: Cuadro Novel (compañía de drama, zarzuela y baile)
O: Zarape nacional, 1 diciembre 1917
La cadena perpetua, 1 diciembre 1917
Granito de sal, 1 diciembre 1917
El novio de Tacha, 18 y 19 abril 1918
Militares de paisano, 18 y 19 abril 1918
El arte de ser bonita, 18 y 19 abril 1918
La viuda alegre, 18 y 19 abril 1918
La walkiria, 18 y 19 abril 1918
La reja de Dolores, 18 y 19 abril 1918
La mujer mexicana, 21 abril 1918
Las bribonas, 20 abril 1918
Hija única, 20 abril 1918
El bateo, 20 abril 1918
Las estrellas, 24 abril 1918
La confesión del indio, 24 abril 1918
Los guapos, 24 abril 1918
El santo de la Isidra, 25 abril 1918
Los chorros del oro, 25 abril 1918
El país de los cartones, 26 abril 1918
Entre doctores, 27 abril 1918
Revista de revistas, 27 abril 1918
El puñado de rosas, 27 abril 1918
La princesa del dólar, 28 abril 1918
El pollo tejada, 28 abril 1918
Lohengrin, 1 mayo 1918
El chiquillo, 1 mayo 1918
El bueno de Guzmán, 1 mayo 1918
Lo que pasa en México, 2 mayo 1918
El puñado de rosas, 4 mayo 1918
Revista alimenticia estomacal, 4 mayo 1918
La cadena perpetua, 4 mayo 1918
El conde de Luxemburgo, 5 mayo 1918
En la hacienda, 5 mayo 1918
La gatita blanca, 5 mayo 1918
N: *El Tucsonense*, 28 noviembre; 5, 12, diciembre 1917; 20 abril 1918

C: Angela Méndez
O: Amor salvaje (de Echegaray)
F: 11 mayo 1918
N: *El Tucsonense*, 11 mayo 1918, p. 4

C: Compañía de Angela Méndez
O: El capitán Marin, 14 mayo 1918
Las riendas del gobierno, 15 mayo 1918
Cuando florezcan los rosales, 16 mayo 1918
La llorona (pieza sentimental), 20 mayo 1918

C: Multicolor
O: Varias zarzuelas y musicales
F: 9 octubre 1918–20 diciembre 1918
N: *El Tucsonense,* 5 octubre 1918, p. 4

C: Compañía dramática Virginia Fábregas
O: Fedora (de Victoriano Sardou)
El cardenal
El mal que nos hacen (de Benavente)
Al amparo de la ley
El genio alegre (de los Hermanos Alvarez Quintero)
F: A partir del 10 diciembre 1918
N: *El Tucsonense,* 7 diciembre 1918

C: Compañía de ópera italiana Graziani-Castillo-Mondragón
O: Lucía de Lammermoor (del maestro Donizetti)
F: 27 marzo 1919
N: *El Tucsonense* (foto), 29 marzo 1919

C: Graziani-Castillo-Mondragón
O: El trovador, 30 marzo 1919
Rigoleto, 28 marzo 1919
Caballería rusticana, 29 marzo 1919
Payasos, 29 marzo 1919
Fausto, 6 abril 1919
La sonámbula, 13 abril 1919

C: María del Carmen Martínez
O: Vida y dulzura, 21 mayo 1919
La madre (de Santiano Ruiseñol), 21 mayo 1919
Para casa de los padres, 21 mayo 1919
Entre doctores, 21 mayo 1919
Chucho el roto, 21 mayo 1919
El pañuelo blanco (de Eusebio Blasco), 21 mayo 1919
Tortosa y soler (graciosa comedia), 21 mayo 1919
La madre (de Santiago Ruiseñol), 3 junio 1919
Para casa de los padres, 4 junio 1919
Los cocineros, 4 junio 1919
Entre doctores, 4 junio 1919
Chucho el roto, 4 junio 1919
La mujer adúltera, 7 junio 1919
Don Juan Tenorio, 8 junio 1919
La llorona, 12 junio 1919
El Grito de Dolores, 13 junio 1919
Revista Pro-patria (de Luis G. de Quevedo, letra de Alonzo Pajares), 17 junio 1919
N: *El Tucsonense* (foto), 20, 29 mayo 1919; 9 junio 1919 (Reseña de "Pro-patria", p. 4)

C: Rosita Arriaga y Gustavo de Lara
O: El último capítulo
El chiquillo (de los Hermanos Quintero)
F: 28 abril 1919
N: *El Tucsonense*, 29 abril 1919

C: Los Perros Comediantes
O: Las bodas de Currito (sainete)
F: 5, 8 y 11 mayo 1919
N: *El Tucsonense*, 3 mayo 1919

C: Mori-Rubi y los Vencedores
O: variedades
F: 12 mayo 1919
N: *El Tucsonense*, 8 mayo 1919

C: Arte Nuevo (compañía de opereta y zarzuela)
O: Los molinos de viento, 29 noviembre 1919
La casta Suzana, 30 noviembre 1919
El asombro de Damasco, 1 diciembre 1919
El soldado de chocolate
La viuda alegre
N: *El Tucsonense*, 29 noviembre 1919 (foto), 2 diciembre 1919

C: Mimí Derba-Caballé (compañía de opereta y zarzuela)
O: El soldado de chocolate, 16 diciembre 1919
La reina del carnaval, 17 diciembre 1919
Las musas del país (zarzuela mexicana), 17 diciembre 1919
Las musas latinas, 18 diciembre 1919
El país de los cartones, 18 diciembre 1919
N: *El Tucsonense*, 18 diciembre 1919

C: Dueto Llera
O: cantables
F: 14 abril 1920 al 18 abril 1920
N: *El Tucsonense*, 13, 15, 17 abril 1920

C: Los Iris (cuadro de zarzuela y variedades)
O: Travesuras de casta, 14 mayo 1920
Mala hembra, 14 mayo 1920
El trébol, 14 mayo 1920
El sueño dorado, 15 mayo 1920
La gran noche, 15 mayo 1920
La banda de trompetas, 15 mayo 1920
N: *El Tucsonense*, 11 mayo 1920 (foto), 15 mayo 1920

C: Campañía de César Sánchez
O: La niña de los besos, 15 diciembre 1920
La rifa galante, 15 diciembre 1920
La tierra de los volcanes, 9 diciembre 1920
La caña morena y la fiebre primaveral, 16 diciembre 1920
Santa, 17 y 19 diciembre 1920

Los campesinos y La isla de los placeres, 18 diciembre 1920
Los molinos de viento y El príncipe carnaval, 19 diciembre 1920
N: *El Tucsonense*, 16, 18, 21 diciembre 1920

C: Los niños Vendrell
O: El sacristán Ropavelas
F: 12 y 13 febrero de 1921
N: *El Tucsonense*, 12 febrero 1921 (anuncio y foto)

C: Hermanos Areu y Bella Oropesa
O: Perro chato (piececita)
Teniendo buen tiempo (piececita)
bailables
F: 16 febrero y 17 febrero 1921
N: *El Tucsonense*, 8 febrero 1921 (anuncio y foto)

C: María del Carmen Martínez
O: Divorciémonos, 25 febrero 1921
La mujer X (drama en 5 actos), 26 febrero 1921
Lluvia de hijos, 1 marzo 1921
La danza de la muerte (drama inglés), 3 marzo 1921
Pro-patria (de Quevedo), 3 marzo 1921

C: Compañía de Drama y Comedia María Teresa Montoya
O: Magda (de Sudderman), 31 marzo 1922
El bastardo o Papá Lebonard, 1 abril 1922
Adiós juventud, 1 abril 1922
La enemiga, 2 abril 1922
La malquerida (de Jacinto Benavente), 4 abril 1922
Zazá, 6 abril 1922
El herrero (de Jorge Ohnet)
N: *El Tucsonense*, 23, 25 (foto), 30 (foto) marzo 1922; 1 (foto), 4, 8 abril 1922

C: Compañía de Espectáculos Modernos (director: Pérez Rodilla)
O: Tierra Baja (de Guimerá), 29 abril 1922
El pobre Valbuena (zarzuela), 29 abril 1922
El país de los cartones, 30 abril 1922
Los pájaros sueltos, 30 abril 1922
El idilio de los viejos, 1 mayo 1922
La gatita (zarzuela), 1 mayo 1922
Trapera y Basta de suegros, 2 mayo 1922
Ya somos tres (zarzuela), 7 mayo 1922
N: *El Tucsonense*, 29 abril 1922 (foto); 2 (foto), 6 mayo 1922

C: Cuadro Romo, Cuadro de variedades
F: 1 julio 1923 y 8 julio 1923
N: *El Tucsonense*, 3 julio 1923

Jorge A. Huerta
University of California-San Diego

The Influences of Latin American Theater on Teatro Chicano

Although much has been written about the development of Chicano theater, and even more has been expressed about the theater of Latin America, it is difficult to find information about the influences of one upon the other. In this study I will attempt to demonstrate that today's Chicano theater reflects a tradition of influence from Latin America that has been almost constant in one form or another since Spanish-language theater first came to this part of the Americas. Furthermore, this tradition has witnessed a flow of creativity from south to north that has included both political and aesthetic considerations. Finally, that influence has been felt in the form of plays, playwrights, directors, actors, musicians and critics who have ventured north to share their visions and expertise.

Beginning with the now legendary performance of a *comedia* by a Capitán Farfán and company on the banks of the Río Chama in 1598, Spanish-language theater has found a home in this country.[1] Though these first *teatristas* were amateurs, and perhaps more Spanish than Mexican, their need to entertain and educate through theatrics became a tradition that Spanish-language churches throughout the United States still practice. Indeed, the Spanish religious folk theater was the most evident theatrical expression in the Southwest for centuries.[2] Initially, then, Spanish-language theater addressed spiritual topics generated by fervent friars who were missionaries before they were playwrights or directors. The influences then were thematic more than technical, for those early productions, like their contemporary counterparts, were strictly community theater at best.

In order to find the more aesthetic influences of Latin America on Chicano theater we must turn to the professional companies that began to tour this country at least by the mid-nineteenth century.[3] According to Nicolás Kanellos, the professional stage had become so established and important to the Spanish-speaking community in California by the

1860s that "companies that once toured the Mexican Republic and abroad, began to settle down to serve as repertory companies" in that state.[4] Because of its proximity, Mexico became the leading supplier of theatrical talent to this country, though there are records of troupes from other countries touring the Spanish-language circuit between 1910 and 1930.[5] Turning again to Kanellos we find that during this period "the clamor for plays written by Mexican writers had increased to such an extent that by 1923 Los Angeles had become a center for Mexican playwriting probably unparalleled in the history of Hispanic communities in the United States."[6]

As Kanellos and other scholars[7] have pointed out, the political nature of today's Chicano theater has its roots in those early companies from Mexico that dramatized sociopolitical issues long before the advent of Luis Valdez's founding of the Teatro Campesino in 1965. This farmworker's theater was the beginning of contemporary Teatro Chicano.[8] And in proclaiming the Teatro Campesino as the moving force behind the theater movement that followed, we leave the boards of the professional stages and turn to a worker's theater, a people's theater that reflects strictly sociopolitical issues in deference to an aesthetic that is well honed or that comes from any source other than expediency coupled with raw, vibrant talent. The course will go full circle, from a people's theater to a professional company, as we follow the progression of the Teatro Campesino and other groups that developed.

Before founding the Teatro Campesino, Luis Valdez wrote a play titled *The Shrunken Head of Pancho Villa* while he was still a student. This play reflected the influence of both Mexican and North American thought and culture as it explored a Mexican/Chicano family's struggle for economic and cultural survival.[9] The play's surrealistic style may have been influenced more by the Europeans than any Latin American playwrights of the time, but the theme owed a great deal to the history of the Mexican people. This play foreshadowed Valdez's interest in *Mexicanismos, pochismos, pachuquismos* and myth—all of which descended from Mexicans residing in the United States.

Another major influence on Valdez's early political development was his trip to Cuba with the first "Venceremos Brigade" in 1964. He returned from that venture with an invigorated enthusiasm for a socialist revolution, proclaiming that Fidel Castro was "the real voice of Latin America," and that social justice must be given to all of Latin America.[10] It was undoubtedly that exposure to the Cuban Revolution that helped inspire Valdez's decision to join a worker's struggle in action, and the first *actos* to emerge from his new group display a definite class analysis.[11] The struggles in Latin America became inspirations for the young man that would soon lead an entire theater movement.

Two years after he formed the Teatro Campesino, Valdez decided to leave the Farmworker's Union and develop both his and his group's theatrical acumen. This difficult decision marked the playwright/director's first step toward a professional theater company. His search for a more developed teatro, as well as his concern with maintaining a cultural identity, led Valdez to investigate the ritual and drama of early Meso-American cultures. The Maya teachings became an inspiration for Valdez's philosophy and his dramaturgy, thus linking him more with Mexican thought and culture than with European or North American values. Certainly, he could not deny the influences of the latter, for he had been born and raised in this country; but Valdez would begin to develop his own mixture of Mayan and Christian mythology, coupled with an aggressive resistance to North American repression in all of its forms.[12]

By 1970 Valdez had written his first *mito*, *Bernabé*,[13] which marked an important turning point for both the playwright and his troupe. This play brought together the history, myth and struggles of the Mexican in this country in a style that might be termed realistic fantasy. Although Valdez's politics had begun to include indigenous thought, he still maintained an interest in Latin America both politically and theatrically. Seeing that there were other teatros developing in this country, and well aware of important theatrical movements in Latin America, Valdez decided to host the first Chicano theater festival in 1970. The Teatro Campesino was definitely the leading teatro of the period on this side of the border, but there were *teatristas* in all parts of Latin America whose expertise could help the developing Chicano groups.

The idea of hosting a festival and inviting groups from Latin America was the first step towards a formal relationship with Latin American theater companies and artists. Initially, the exchange was limited to the participation of fifteen groups, including El Nuevo Teatro Pobre de las Américas of Puerto Rico and El Grupo de Poesía Coral de Mascarones of Mexico City. Mariano Leyva, director of the Mexican troupe, emerged from the 1970 festival as a leading director and spokesperson among Chicano theaters for the struggles in his country and in all of Latin America. His youthful company performed a very disciplined and effective form of choral poetry which had not been seen before in the teatro movement. Leyva's troupe was an important link with the Chicano's linguistic heritage, bringing the Spanish language to life for a people whose linguistic particularities had been a political drawback since the instrusion of the Anglo. Teatro de los Barrios of San Antonio, Texas, wrote a piece about the Alamo in the style of choral poetry as a result of the Mascarones' successful example.[14]

Mariano Leyva became the first of many Latin American directors who would have interaction with the Chicanos after the initial festival, and his influence on the emerging coalition of teatros, named El Teatro Nacional de Aztlán (TENAZ) in 1971, is still evident.[15] Leyva and his troupe had quickly won the respect and admiration of the Chicanos, for they seemed much more disciplined and dedicated to their art and politics; it was therefore very meaningful that he should assert the following at the first TENAZ Director's Conference in 1971: *"Tenemos que crear un teatro revolucionario . . . tenemos que aprovechar el teatro de otros como los griegos."*[16] During this early period in the development of the teatro movement, it would have been useless for a director from the traditional commodity theater to proclaim that the Chicanos should or could get anything out of the Greeks and their theater. But coming from a man like Leyva, whose commitment to a popular theater was evident, the suggestion could be taken seriously and with respect. None of the *teatristas* of the time ran to their public libraries to get copies of Sophocles or Aristophanes, but an important seed was planted, a suggestion that would find its time ten years later.

In 1973, four years after the first festival, the teatros gathered in San Jose, California, to continue their annual investigation and sharing of ideas. One production stood out as indicative of the differences between typical Chicano *actos* and a more symbolic Latin American dramaturgy, *Moloch*, by Rodolfo Santana of Venezuela. Santana had worked with students of Susana Castillo at the University of California at Los Angeles, who took Santana's play to San Jose. The tale of Moloch, half-man, half-bull, was rife with symbolism and metaphor—dramatic elements that had heretofore eluded the basic *actos* and other dramatic statements coming from the Chicanos.

During the next day's critique panel there was much discussion and debate about the efficacy of a play as symbolic as *Moloch*. "Would *campesinos* understand this?" asked one observer, to which Mariano Leyva replied that the work was more for *"la pequeña burguesía."*[17] The reaction was decidedly mixed, but the nature of the debate indicated that Santana's dramaturgy had reached beyond the basics of Teatro Chicano; and there were few *teatristas* from this side of the border that could relate to the work and its symbolism. Not as a defense, but as a clarification, Santana told the lively crowd of participants that he had tried to relate the violence and misery of Venezuela's slums. Certainly, there were those in attendance who saw the symbolism and were excited by it, but it was clear that Santana's vision was meant for more sophisticated observers. Most importantly, the *teatristas* had been exposed to Santana's developing dramaturgy and could extract from it the knowledge that conditions in each country were distinct and had to be dealt with on different levels.

When the Chicanos in TENAZ ventured to Mexico City for "El Quinto Festival de los Teatros Chicanos, Primer Encuentro Latinoamericano" in June of 1974, the event had international repercussions.[18] Here were the Chicanos and Latin Americans meeting in Mexico, conducting performances, workshops and critique sessions that were both stimulating and frustrating. Debates raged over productions such as Luis Valdez's *Gran carpa de los Rasquachis*, but ultimately the confrontations were necessary stepping-stones to a much more important alliance between the groups from *"un continente y una cultura."* This festival proved that the cultures really were distinct; but, although the conditions in each country were different as well, good theater would ultimately be the major indicator of a teatro's success.

Groups such as the Teatro Experimental de Cali, La Candelaria, La Mamá and Los Mascarones, to name a few, could not but leave their impressions on one another and on the younger groups from the United States. This festival provided a rare instance of the Chicanos going to the Latin Americans, as it were, but after the festival, several groups and individuals followed the Chicanos home. The earlier tradition of traveling troupes coming to this country from Latin America was revived, and this time they brought both politics and aesthetics to the barrios. Most importantly, however, directors and playwrights began to come here to offer workshops and to direct works, sometimes at universities, often with teatros, and also with the emerging small professional companies, particularly in Los Angeles. A "theatrical diaspora" emerged from the 1974 festival; it began a limited but effective crossover of ideas and talent.

By the mid-1970s, the Teatro Movement had developed on three distinct levels: student/community groups, the full-time Teatro Campesino and professionally oriented groups. At each of these levels the influence of Latin American *teatristas* is notable. At the university level playwrights such as Emilio Carballido have contributed to a developing Chicano dramaturgy, conducting playwriting workshops and directing the products of those classes. Carballido has taught at various institutions in this country, including California State University at Los Angeles.

During Carballido's tenure at Los Angeles, his class produced original scripts which prompted Professor Romulus Zamora to observe, "Carballido taught his students how to do poor theater artistically . . . he made the edges of the roughness soft."[19] Indeed, Zamora is one notable example of how the playwright influenced Chicano work; he produced Carballido's *Yo también hablo de la rosa* at California State University at Sacramento in 1980. The distinguished Mexican playwright has also participated at several teatro festivals in recent years, adding his astute vision to critique panels and playwriting sessions.

Another playwright who has influenced the direction of Chicano theater through his work is Osvaldo Dragún. This Argentine playwright's *Historias para ser contadas* has been produced in part or in its entirety by several Chicano groups in this country. Under the direction of Adrián Vargas, Teatro de la Gente adapted the "Hombre que se convirtió en perro" segment of the *Historias*, expanding the playlet into a full-length statement about Mexican and Chicano workers who were losing their jobs in local industry. The conversion from man to canine was set in a *corrido* style, using popular ballads to musically narrate the story.[20] Dragún brought his own company to this country in the late '70s and produced the *Historias*, undoubtedly having a direct influence on those *teatristas* who saw the production.

Enrique Buenaventura's influence has been felt through his participation at festivals, his group's performances and his plays. Teatro de la Esperanza first met Buenaventura and his troupe at a theater festival in San Francisco, California, in 1972 and remained dedicated followers of both TEC and their playwright-director. In 1980 this teatro produced *La orgía* as an experiment for its local audience under the direction of José Vacas of Ecuador. This is an example of a full-time teatro working with a Latin American director in producing a Latin American play. And if we include the fact that two of the actors were Mexicans, the connection is complete. When asked what their audiences felt about the play, members of the Santa Barbara troupe sadly replied, "They just couldn't understand it,"[21] echoing the remarks about *Moloch* several years earlier. Nonetheless, the experiment with Buenaventura's play was beneficial to the actors in both craft and play analysis. *La orgía* prepared the Teatro for its next collective creation, *The Octopus*, and Mr. Vacas also made his mark, staging several scenes.

Another director whose influence has touched several groups in this country is Humberto Martínez of Argentina, now with the Instituto Nacional de Bellas Artes of Mexico City. Martínez conducted workshops in Los Angeles and San Jose in the late '70s and was instrumental in encouraging actors in those communities to seek further training. While working in San Jose, Martínez introduced Teatro de la Gente to Latin American plays such as the *Historias* and also directed the teatro and community members in the Chilean folk canatata *The Siege of Santa María de Iquiqui*. In the words of José Saucedo, a founding member of Teatro de la Esperanza, "Humberto helped put the Chicano struggle on an international level, blending politics with art."[22]

Another very active director, Carlos Barón of Chile, has been a moving force in the Latino theater of San Francisco for the last several years. Barón directs Teatro Latino in San Francisco's Mission District, a cosmopolitan community of Latinos, Chicanos and Mexicans that reflects a much more discerning audience than most working-class barrios, perhaps because so many of the residents are educated expatriots from all over Latin America. Along with adapting and directing *La orgía* and mounting a musical piece about Lolita Lebrón, Barón seemingly took the words of Mariano Leyva to heart (though Barón was not at the first meeting) and adapted Aristophanes' *Lysistrata* to the current problem of barrio warfare. Re-titled *Liz Estrada*, this Greek classic successfully demonstrated how a universal statement against war could be creatively adapted by a judicious playwright.

Along with the playwrights, directors, critics and actors who have made their mark on the teatro movement, we must not forget the music of Latin America. Beginning with the already mentioned Mexican *corrido*, music has always been an integral part of Chicano theater. It was only natural for the Latin American protest songs as well as indigenous music to become a part of the Chicano's dramatic statements as well. Many teatros include this music in their presentations, either as musical prologue or within the plays themselves. Teatro de la Esperanza, for example, adapted several pieces from *The Siege of Santa María de Iquiqui* in their documentary *Guadalupe* in 1974, altering the lyrics to suit the needs of the play.[23]

Finally, we turn to the emerging professional theater groups that attempt to address the issues of the barrios within their repertoires. In Los Angeles, the prime example of a professional theater company is the Bilingual Foundation of the Arts. Founded by Chicana actress, Carmen Zapata, the Cuban-born director, Margarita Galbán, the BFA has been very instrumental in bringing the works of Latin American playwrights to the Chicano communities. Galbán directed a stunning production of *Los soles truncos* in 1980 which was produced both in Los Angeles and New York City. René Marqués's play, so deftly acted and directed, made its impact on the *teatristas*, demonstrating what can be said in a realistic style. Some members of Los Angeles-based teatros have worked with Ms. Galbán in classes as well as productions, adding immeasurably to their training.

The progression from a people's theater to a professionally oriented company is not the norm among the teatros. Indeed, only the Teatro Campesino can be termed a fully professional troupe now that it has become California's sixth Equity company. The Teatro's alliance with the Actor's Equity Association guarantees the incomes of the company, but it also harbors financial commitments far beyond those of the early years. The Esperanza group is the only other full-time teatro, meaning the members do not earn their livelihoods from any other activity, but their pay is minimal and their commitment constantly tested under adverse living conditions. The BFA works with professional actors from a large pool of Latino talent in Hollywood, but this group cannot afford to pay salaries.

Beyond all this—the groups that range from students to fully-trained professionals—lies the fact that few institutions of higher learning are addressing the needs of the Chicano community. Conditions are not much better in the theater arts departments, yet it is clear that the only avenue for effective growth is through training in the academies. To date much of the training that *teatristas* in this country have received has come from practical experience, a few drama departments and, notably, from the many individuals and groups beyond the few listed on these pages. Mention has been made of the Chicano audience's lack of sophistication, but it is important to note the lack of training at all levels among the *teatristas* themselves.

As the diaspora of groups that come to this country continues to grow and evolve, a very significant event occurred in the spring of 1982: Cuba's Grupo Escambray's tour of the United States. The Escambray's visit marks the beginning of what could be the most significant interchange yet for teatros in recent history. Here for the first time a theater group toured from a country that supports its *teatristas* both financially and spiritually. Rather than the "starving artists" we have become so accustomed to greeting at our borders, the Escambray's staff came to us well-fed. Their art is also the result of good training, a training that the Chicanos have yet to receive in any great numbers.

The Escambray's tour was preceded by a trip to Cuba by *teatristas* from this country in the summer of 1981. The thirty participants in this historic event saw a revolution in progress and learned that teatro is a noble profession. This brigade will be followed by others and one hopes by an exchange of teatros as well. Plans are under way for Teatro de la Esperanza to perform in Cuba in December of 1982, and we are looking for avenues to bring directors and other *teatristas* to this country for residencies in our institutions. It is probably no accident that we should turn to Cuba for guidance and training. This move recalls the period of the 1920s and '30s when theater artists from this country traveled to Russia to learn about their craft and returned to form the foundation of today's professional theater.

It is evident by now that the diaspora flows northward from Latin America. If there is going to be a change in this pattern, then the Chicanos are going to have to arm themselves with the necessary training, both artistic and political, to have something to offer our more sophisticated *compañeros* to the south. [24] The presence of a professional company of actors that has not denied its community—that is very much a part of a worker's struggle—is going to leave its mark in our communities. With the continued support of our colleagues in Latin America, Chicano theater will continue to develop its aesthetic and its audiences, and the exchange will become equal.

[1] Winifred Johnson, "Early Theater in the Spanish Borderlands," *Mid-America* 13 (October 1930), 125.

[2] See (Sister) Joseph Marie McCrossan, *The Role of the Church and the Folk in the Development of the Early Drama in New Mexico* (Philadelphia, 1948) for more on the Spanish religious folk theater.

[3] From an unpublished ms. in the author's collection by Nicolás Kanellos, *The*

Origins and Development of Hispanic Theatre in the Southwest, p. 4.

[4] Kanellos, p. 4.

[5] Kanellos, p. 10.

[6] Kanellos, p. 11.

[7] See John Brokaw, "A Mexican-American Acting Company, 1849-1924," Educational Theatre Journal 17 (March 1975), 23-29; John Brokaw, "The Repertory of a Mexican-American Theatrical Troupe: 1849-1924," Latin American Theatre Review 8 (Fall 1974), 25-35; and Jorge A. Huerta, Chicano Theatre: Themes and Forms (Ypsilanti: Bilingual Press, 1982), 157.

[8] For more on the development of the Teatro Campesino see: Beth Bagby, "El Teatro Campesino: Interviews with Luis Valdez," Tulane Drama Review 11 (Summer 1967), 56-62; Sylvie Drake, "Keeping the Revolution on Stage," Performing Arts Magazine (September 1970), 56-62; John Harrop and Jorge A. Huerta, "The Agit-Prop Pilgrimage of Luis Valdez and El Teatro Campesino," Theatre Quarterly 5 (March-May 1975), 30-39; Jorge A. Huerta, "Chicano Agit-Prop: The Early Actos of El Teatro Campesino," LATR 11 (Spring 1977), 45-58; and Huerta, Chicano Theatre, 12-27.

[9] The Shrunken Head of Pancho Villa has yet to be published. For a description of this play, see Betty Diamond, Brown Eyed Children of the Sun: The Cultural Politics of El Teatro Campesino (Ann Arbor: University Microfilms, 1977), 129-146; and Huerta, Chicano Theatre, 49-60.

[10] Stan Steiner and Luis Valdez, Aztlán: An Anthology of Mexican-American Literature (New York: Vintage Books, 1972), 218.

[11] See Las dos caras del patroncito and La quinta temporada in Luis Valdez's Actos (San Juan Bautista: Cucaracha Press, 1971), 7-34.

[12] Luis Valdez, Pensamiento Serpentino (San Juan Bautista: Cucaracha Press, 1973); also in Chicano Theatre One (primavera 1973), 7-19.

[13] Roberto J. Garza, Contemporary Chicano Theatre (Notre Dame: University of Notre Dame Press, 1976), 30-58; scene three of Bernabé is in Steiner and Valdez, Aztlán, 361-376.

[14] El Alamo: What Really Happened is an unpublished ms. by Teatro de los Barrios, San Antonio, in the author's collection.

[15] Indeed, it was Leyva who suggested the name "TENAZ" for the new organization. Unfortunately, the Mascarones split up in 1979 and Leyva faded into the background of TENAZ.

[16] From the author's notes of the TENAZ Director's Meeting, held in Fresno, California, April 17, 1971.

[17] From the author's notes of the festival, June 21, 1973, San Jose, California. See also Susana Castillo, "Cuarto Festival de Teatros Chicanos en San Jose, Califas," LATR 7 (Fall 1973), 100-102; David Copelin, "Chicano Theatre: El Festival de los Teatros Chicanos," The Drama Review 17 (December 1973), 86-89.

[18] For reports of this festival see: Susana Castillo, "Festivales de Teatro en America," LATR 8 (Fall 1974), 75-78; Teresa González, "Quinto Festival de los Teatros Chicanos/Primer Encuentro Latinoamericano," Caracol 1 (September 1974), 3-7; and Theodore Shank, "A Return to Aztec and Maya Roots," The Drama Review 18 (December 1974), 56-70.

[19] From an interview with Romulus Zamora, March 6, 1982, Cardiff-by-the-Sea, California.

[20] Jorge A. Huerta, Chicano Theatre, 27-36.

[21] From an interview with Evelina Fernández, José Saucedo and José Luis Valenzuela, of Teatro de la Esperanza, March 6, 1982, Cardiff-by-the-Sea, California.

[22] From the interview on March 6, 1982.

[23] Guadalupe will soon be published by Chicano Studies Publications, University of California, San Diego.

[24] Some teatristas from this country have lectured and conducted workshops in Latin

America. The author of this article visited Panama, Mexico City and Caracas on a State Department tour in 1977 and conducted a week-long workshop in the Dominican Republic in 1980. However, trips of this nature are too brief and often suspect because of the U.S.I.C.A. affiliation, and therefore not as productive as they could be. Most recently, José Saucedo spent several months in Venezuela and Colombia studying the theater there, and certainly sharing his knowledge of Chicano theater, but the experience should be shared by many more people.

Yvonne Yarbro-Bejarano
University of Washington

Teatropoesía by Chicanas in the Bay Area: *Tongues of Fire*

Recently, the so-called "crisis" in Chicano theater has generated a great deal of discussion. Those who attended the 11th Chicano Theater Festival, sponsored by TENAZ (el Teatro Nacional de Aztlán), the official organization of Chicano theater groups, were alarmed at the small number of Chicano teatros participating.[1] In July 1982 the seminar meeting of TENAZ in San Diego was dedicated in part to airing the problems surrounding the seventeen-year-old theater movement as well as possible solutions. In this atmosphere of arrested development and dwindling resources, the vitality of women in theater is truly noteworthy. Of the handful of non-Latin American groups performing at the last Festival, held in San Francisco in September 1981, two were companies made up entirely of women: Teatro Raíces of San Diego headed by Felicita Núñez and Valentina Productions, Inc. of San Jose. At the present time, the most important positions in TENAZ are filled by women: Lily Delgadillo is the new chair, Evelina Fernández, the artistic co-ordinator, and a new position has been created to deal specifically with women's issues, held by Carolina Flores. At the most recent TENAZ meeting, which took place in November 1982 in San Francisco's Mission District, it was decided that the *TENAZ Talks Teatro*, the newsletter disseminating information about teatro, would be put together by Hank Tavera and published in *La Revista Literaria de El Tecolote* in San Francisco and would feature a column on women in teatro by Cara Hill de Castañón. I would like to focus this discussion of women's present role in theater on a specific geographic area—California's Bay Area— where the theatrical activity of women is particularly effervescent, and concentrate on a specific form which is finding special favor among them: *teatropoesía*.

The popularity of this form may be explained in various ways. The lack of Chicano playwrights is notorious and is often cited as one of the contributing factors in the decline of Chicano theater. In *teatropoesía*

Chicanas have discovered a creative way to skirt this problem. While they are committed to dealing with women's issues in teatro, most have no playwriting skills. Writing poetry involves less technical training, making it an accessible vehicle for the direct expression of emotions and experience. Given the repertory of Chicano plays available, many women prefer their own or other women's poetry to scripts that are geared to men's perspective and relegate women to minor or stereotyped roles. Others see *teatropoesía* as a means of connecting with the veritable explosion of talent manifested in the poetry being written by Chicanas. By carrying these texts to the stage, women in theater can expose them to another kind of audience that would not ordinarily read poetry. *Teatropoesía* exploits the beauty and power of words, a dimension often neglected in Chicano theater, combining the compact directness and lyrical emotion of the poetic text with the physical immediacy of the three-dimensional work of theater. In this fusion of two media, the verbal, private word of the printed text is translated into action in time and space, directly experienced as sight and sound. The silent dialogue between lone reader and poem has been replaced by communication that is collective, social and public in nature.

While the majority of Chicano teatros have worked with the *acto* form in various stages of development,[2] *teatropoesía*, the creative fusion of drama and poetic texts, does have some history within the Chicano theater movement. In 1974, Dorinda Moreno and Las Cucarachas performed *Chicana*, a blend of dance, poetry, music and prose, first for a minifestival in San Francisco's Mission District and then in Mexico during the Quinto Festival. In a pamphlet prepared for the Festival, the group, based in San Francisco, defined itself as a "mezcla teatral de mujeres," whose goals included: "perpetuar la vida familiar y también dar a conocer las mujeres indio/latinas que pasaron a la Historia por la liberación de su pueblo." The piece combined the image of woman as "Mother Earth," symbol of fertility and mainstay of the strong, united family, with the "mujer rebelde" who demands equality with men and participates actively in social and political struggles. Among the figures evoked in the poems, songs and dances were *la indígena* of pre-Columbian times, the Native American, La Adelita of the Mexican Revolution, La Llorona, a Brazilian mother accusing her government of repression and genocide, and "la nueva Chicana."

In 1979, two members of the Teatro Campesino, Oliva Chumacero and Rogelio "Smiley" Rojas, presenting themselves as *teatropoetas*, performed a piece called *Cabuliando in Motion* for community groups and agencies in San Juan Bautista, Merced, the San Joaquin Valley and Stanford. They had been writing poetry on and off before 1979. Being theater people, they balked at the idea of simply "reading" the poems to an audience and developed a theatrical rendering of the texts. The theme of the presentation was the cycle of life from both the female and the male perspectives. The various phases of the cycle led into one another, beginning with birth and childhood, passing through adulthood, including healthy doses of sociopolitical satire, and ending with death. The elaboration of the material illustrated both the attraction and the challenge of *teatropoesía*. The middle part of the piece presented the most difficulties, dealing with love and love relationships. These poems were the hardest to translate into action, whereas the beginning and the end were perceived as highly charged with dramatic energy. These poems lent themselves well to visual action and theatrics, for example, the fireblowing which signaled the "end." The title of the piece captures the essence of *teatropoesía*'s fusion of two genres, "cabuleo" meaning barrio talk or play with words "in motion." The couple is considering working up another *teatropoesía* presentation, this time including the work of the best documented Nahuatl poet, Netzahualcoyotl, and that of José Antonio Burciaga and others.[3]

Beginning in the Fall of 1981 and continuing to the present there has been a remarkable resurgence of *teatropoesía* by women in the Bay Area. The first of these efforts was *Voz de la mujer*, a polished collage of poetry, music, dance and pantomime presented by Valentina Productions of San Jose during the 11th TENAZ Festival. Valentina grew out of the very active group of women working within TENAZ, specifically out of W.I.T. (Women in Teatro), founded in 1978 to address women's issues. Five members of Valentina performed the work: Irene Burgos, Rosie Campos-Pantoja, Cara Hill de Castañón, Liz Robinson and Juanita Vargas plus Anita Mattos, a member of Teatro Latino in San Francisco. The show received an overwhelmingly positive response, as did the objectives of the group itself, dedicated to the exploration of women through theater. In form and content, *Voz de la mujer* was reminiscent of *Chicana* by Las Cucarachas, also performed within the context of a TENAZ festival. The show began with a presentation of the Chicana's historical antecedents: an Aztec dance, Sor Juana of Colonial times, the Adelita. With regard to women's experience, as does *Chicana*, *Voz de la mujer* emphasized male/female relationships and the exaltation of motherhood. Shortly after the performance, the majority of the members left the group, beset from the beginning with a number of economic, ideological and personal problems. The two remaining members, Irene Burgos and Liz Robinson, performed a ten-minute segment of *Voz* in December 1981 for The Grail, a women's organization in San Jose. Most of the original members have recently begun to meet again, with the added injection of enthusiasm represented by Carolina Flores' presence in San Jose; but they see themselves primarily as a support group for women in theater, providing a forum to work out physically and exchange ideas, with no immediate plans for mounting a show.

The second *teatropoesía* event in the Bay Area was *Tongues of Fire*, which arose in circumstances very different from those which produced *Voz de la mujer*. While Valentina originated as a support group that eventually felt the need to mount a production, *Tongues of Fire* was originally conceived of and performed as a component of the Cultural Heritage of Chicana Literature conference held in Oakland in October 1981. The conference was co-sponsored by Aztlán Cultural, an Arts Service Organization made up in part by Roberta Fernández, Roberta Orona and Lucha Corpi, and the Latin American Projects Committee of the Oakland Museum, and funded by a grant from the California Council for the Humanities. Lucha Corpi was in charge of the organizational and administrative aspects of the *teatropoesía* project. With the basic idea and form already conceptualized—a stage reading of Chicana poetry covering a broad range of representative topics—Aztlán Cultural approached Barbara Brinson-Pineda to put together a script. Antonio Curiel, a doctoral student in drama at Stanford who has conducted theater workshops in the Bay Area, was contracted to direct the show. The four actresses included two of the original members of Valentina: Rosie Campos, a dancer who also toured with San Jose's Teatro de la Gente, and Cara Hill de Castañón, whose experience spans more than seven years and includes work with Teatro Latino and Teatro de la Gente. The other two actresses were Carolina Juárez, folklorist and teacher who majored in drama at Arizona State University, and Teresa Romero-Rivera, actress and visual artist. The show was performed the evening of the final day of the conference to an audience which included participants in the conference as well as many people from the community and friends and family of the people involved in the project.[4]

For Cinco de Mayo 1982 in San Jose, Cara Hill *No me callarán, no me callaré*, a recreation of the life of Sor Juana Inés dela Cruz based entirely on her own words. Electra Arenal, a *mexicana* from New York, put the script together using excerpts from Sor Juana's poetry and prose, especially the *Respuesta . . . a Sor Filotea*. The actress is in the process of reviving the show for more performances.

Currently, there are at least four *teatropoesía* projects underway in the Bay Area. Cara Hill and Anita Mattos are preparing a show for the 12th TENAZ Festival, scheduled for Spring 1983 in Los Angeles. The piece, called "Poetisas de América," will include the works of such writers as Violeta Parra, Lolita Lebrón and Julia de Burgos. In addition to songs, with music provided by Cuauhtémoc Castañón, the actresses plan to dramatize the importance of these women's lives. At Stanford, drama student Marta Carrillo is preparing a performance of the poetry of Juan Felipe Herrera and has become very active with the women in theater in TENAZ and around the Bay Area. In the Mission District of San Francisco several women have decided to form a group to culminate many years of working together in a neighborhood context, including Chicanas and other Third-World women. Inspired by conceptual artist Susan Lacey, they would like to break with the traditional styles of Chicano theater and present a surrealistic *teatropoesía* piece, combining poetry, abstract modern dance and prerecorded audio. Highly symbolic in style, the show would recreate women's internal struggle with conflicting parts of the self, depicted by the four actresses Natalia Ceballos, Marta Estrella, Regina Mounton and Lisa Ramírez, each using four masks created by Amalia Mesa Baines in the Kabuki style. The "death" brought about by the collision of these emotions and energies leads to the rebirth of the new woman, represented as a kind of creator god figure. The group has been working since October 1982 and plans to schedule the show around Easter 1983 to enhance the theme of rebirth. Another new group, also in the Mission District, grew out of political work with Casa Nicaragua and Casa El Salvador. The three women, Eva Cháidez, María Rosa Galdames and *salvadoreña* Cecilia Guidos, began working in Fall 1982 on teatro fusing women's issues and the situation in El Salvador, based on Guidos' poetry. They plan to combine this technique with the three-frame structure of the political comic strip.[5]

From this brief review, it is clear that women represent a vital and creative force within Chicano theater that covers a broad range of styles, perspectives and organizational affiliations. The following analysis of *Tongues of Fire* is offered as one example of the kind of work Chicanas are doing in *teatropoesía* in the Bay Area and the kind of images of women they are projecting.

The key to successful *teatropoesía* is the selection of strong poems, which in turn requires a certain knowledge of Chicana poetry. Ideally, all theater people dramatizing certain issues in their plays should strive to keep in touch with the research or creative writing other Chicanos are doing on the same subject. In practice, Chicano scholars and artists tend to isolate themselves in their particular disciplines. The strength of *Tongues of Fire* lies in its successful combination of theatrical experience, literary training and familiarity with recent publications by Chicana feminists. While the members of Valentina came to *teatropoesía* primarily as theater workers, Brinson-Pineda approached theater as a poet who has been widely anthologized and who has authored a book of poetry, *Nocturno*. She is also a member of the Board of Milagro Books, which distributes Chicano literature, and is well-versed in Chicano poetry and in the literary movement in general. Besides her poetry, she has written reviews of plays and books for *La Revista Literaria de El Tecolote*. Her theater experience dates back to 1978, when she was asked to write a script for a class on bilingual theater at Mills College. The play, *Guadalupe*, based on the myth of the Virgin's appearance to

82

Juan Diego, was performed at Mills and other places in the Bay Area. The result of Brinson-Pineda's familiarity with Chicana poetry is a strong script. *Tongues of Fire* is an excellent sampling of some of the best texts from our most vigorous and creative writers. At the same time, the production showed that effective *teatropoesía* must combine strong text with theatrical sensibility. The selection of poems ultimately depended on how well they lent themselves to staging and whether they communicated well orally. Curiel's role was crucial in the translation of the poems into the language of theater. In the quality of the script and its successful theatrical rendering, *Tongues of Fire* is a good example of *teatropoesía*'s innovative cross fertilization between two different genres of Chicano literature.

The structure of *Tongues of Fire* is distinctly more literary than that of *Voz de la mujer*. The latter show reveals its links with TENAZ in the use of the "historical procession" format, interspersed with songs and dances, familiar to all students of the Chicano theater movement. The Teatro Campesino, the Mascarones from Mexico, and many other groups have presented dramatic representations of Chicano history, from pre-Columbian times, through the Conquest to modern *mestizo* reality. *Voz* adopted this format to show the struggles of women in history as well as in their daily lives. Brinson-Pineda opted for a loose grouping of poems around various themes in five sections. The unifying thread which ties the sections together is the idea of the Chicana writer. The exploration of the goals and dreams of the Chicana writer and the problems facing her makes *Tongues of Fire* a truly groundbreaking effort in the projection of images of women in Chicano theater. In their development of this theme, Brinson-Pineda and Curiel hooked up with the most recent thinking and writing of Chicana feminists, published in *This Bridge Called My Back*, a powerful collection of essays and poems by radical women of color, edited by Gloria Anzaldúa and Cherríe Moraga.[6] In her review of *This Bridge* for *La Revista Literaria*,[7] Brinson-Pineda characterized it as a significant step in the definition of feminism by women of color, focusing on the importance of culture and class and directly confronting the charged issues of homophobia and racism within the women's movement.

"Collage in Brown," the first section of *Tongues of Fire*, deals with the consciousness of the writer, specifically the Chicana writer. A women sits at a table, writing. This image is maintained throughout the show. In each section, a different actress sat writing at the table until each one had had a chance to play the role of the writer. As if reading from the pages she is working on, the actress playing the writer in "Collage of Brown" recites fragments of poems which touch on the theme of writing. The other three actresses are positioned around her, and dialogue with her and with each other using texts taken from a piece published in *This*

Bridge, "Speaking in Tongues: A Letter to Third World Women Writers" by Gloria Anzaldúa. "Collage in Brown" presents the major themes and the ideological focus of *Tongues of Fire* as a whole. Brinson-Pineda selected succinct passages from "Speaking in Tongues" which focus on the precise nature of the struggle of the Chicana writer, a struggle inseparable from her experience of triple oppression on the grounds of sex, race and class. The Chicana's color exacerbates the feelings of inadequacy and self-hatred instilled in all females by a sexist society. These feelings of inferiority are further compounded by a long history of economic and racial oppression which has held the Chicana in menial, often backbreaking jobs and systematically denied her access to literacy. But learning to write and convincing herself that she can write and has something worthwhile to say is only half the battle. One of the fundamental themes of *Tongues of Fire* is the need for the Chicana writer to cultivate her own voice, and not merely learn to write like the white middle class. The point is immediately and forcefully made in "Collage in Brown" in a quote from "Speaking in Tongues" which holds the key to the title of the show: "The white man speaks: Perhaps if you scrape the dark off your face. Maybe if you bleach your bones. Stop speaking in tongues, stop writing left-handed. Don't cultivate your colored skins nor tongues of fire if you want to make it in a right-handed world." Her sex, her culture and her class, which place obstacles in the path of the Chicana writer, must ultimately become the source of her strength, the "deep core" from which she writes. Through her writing the Chicana explores her personal and collective identity; her voice speaks for those who have been silenced.

All but one of the poem fragments in "Collage in Brown" reappear in their entirety in other sections. They represent a poetic development of the major points of the narrative taken from the essay "Speaking in Tongues" which form the thematic heart of the show. The fragment from "when all the yous," by Veronica Cunningham, talks about the difficulty in overcoming deep-seated inhibitions about writing for and about women. "Visions of Mexico While at a Writing Symposium in Port Townsend, Washington," by Lorna Dee Cervantes,[8] is one of the cornerstone texts of *Tongues of Fire*. The segments from this poem recited in the first section highlight the Chicana's sense of historical connection as a major source of strength as a writer. The poetic voice passionately affirms her descent from "a long line of eloquent illiterates / whose history reveals what words don't say. / Our anger is our way of speaking, / the gesture is an utterance more pure than word." At the same time she expresses her need to dominate the written word in order to destroy stereotypes about her people and to rewrite history from the perspective of the oppressed. Emy López' "Orgánico" harmonizes with the theme of the poem as a document of a people which persists beyond the lifetime of the individual and touches briefly and movingly on the intimate search for transcendence and immorality through writing: "quedará / de mí / únicamente / un poema / una pequeña parte / mi tierra cruda."[9] The only complete poem in this section, and the only one not repeated in any other, "Quedarse quieto" by Lucha Corpi, confronts the overwhelming temptation not to write, which would mean an escape from pain but ultimately the acceptance of impotence. The poem is an exhortation to meet the challenge of the first blank page: "Quedarse quieto / es no hallar el dolor / de tu carne / y de tu aliento / y sí encontrar la tiranía / de los huesos calcinados / por el sol negro / de nuestras impotencias."[10]

"Collage in Brown" sets the tone for the whole; the following four sections explore the struggle of the Chicana writer to transform weakness into strength, by seeking out and affirming her collective and familial history, by challenging social, cultural and sexual oppression and by giving full expression to her visions and dreams.

The second section, "The Past within Us," further developes the theme of the importance of history, especially the experience of women, in the life of the contemporary Chicana. The point of view is that of two women in the past: the poetic voice of "Arriaga" by Shylda Alvarez and that of "María la O" by Barbara Brinson-Pineda.[11] The two long poems were delivered as interlocking monologues by two actresses positioned in separate areas of the stage, addressing the audience and each other. "María la O" tells the intimate history of one woman's migration from Mexico to the fields of the United States. After a loveless childhood of harshness and poverty, María finds happiness when she marries Mario. That their happiness will be shortlived is foreshadowed by the pet lamb which they inadvertently crush between them one night, "searching for each other in dreams." Mario falls ill, and the imagery becomes an ominous parody of the earlier eroticism of the poem: "A devil / perches on Mario's chest, / wings shadow lungs. / Its tongue on my love's tongue, / it sucks his breath." When Mario dies, María's mother writes for her to join them in El Paso. The lovers' embrace has been definitively broken and replaced by death and necessity: "My love's cold arms hold / Death to his breast. / The straight steel arms of the train track / will embrace me." The poem ends with a vision of the migratory cycle which will be María's future: "Texas cotton, Michigan cherry, / California grape, / to the city's concrete bed, / to an open road."

"Arriaga," set in Mexico in 1933, contrasts a young girl's experience at a convent boarding school in San Luis with her summers at home in the village Arriaga. The poem is structured on alternating rhythms of restriction and release, repression or bondage, literal and figurative, and escape, physical and mental. At the convent boarding school she sleeps, "under the nun's eyes / my hands holding down a white sheet /

to keep them from fluttering from beneath." The drone of endless chants and rosaries becomes the medium which "lets me fly beyond the prayers / to the grazing land on the crest of a hill" of Arriaga. When she is released from the pure and sheltered world of the boarding school ("I wait for the opening / of the convent rail gate"), she runs to the world of Arriaga, a world steeped in the life of the senses which is at once repulsive and attractive to her. The girl runs past the crumbling adobe houses, the carcass surrounded with flies and the "hollow-faced women / wrapped in black shawls" of the marketplace, but also past the bakery, "with bread that smells of warm flesh / closer than a thousand prayers." Here also in Arriaga the girl is subjected to discipline and restrictions: she must work, and among her duties is waiting on the ranchers, "men who will hook their eyes on my body / who will slip a rough hand beneath my dress." Struggling to master the art of needlecraft, the girl fears failure, which she can escape in mental flight ("I can give up and fly / to the sound of nuns chanting") or in her budding sexuality ("but if I give up / to the flutter of hands beneath my dress"), which she knows will bring punishment: "she will bind my hands and legs / to a chair / to think white." The poem concludes with the image of the girl bound physically and mentally by roles and attitudes determined before her birth, as she contemplates freedom in the voices of the children playing, in the grazing land "that lies like a promise / before the front door," in the soaring flight of her imagination: "breathe, breathe / watch the clouds do slow somersaults / in the afternoon air."

"The Past within Us" presents a sensitive exploration of the experience of women in Mexico belonging to the generation of the poets' mothers or grandmothers. It provides the opportunity to meditate on continuity and change, on how our own lives have been shaped but yet differ from the experiences of women like María and the girl of Arriaga.

All the action of the third section of the show, "Plática de sobremesa," takes place in the kitchen. The title recalls relaxed conversations at the table after dinner with family and friends. In Chicano families the kitchen is the center of family activities and the scene of the most intimate conversations. While the *sala* is reserved for more formal visits or for people for whom it is important to keep up appearances, the family and closest friends gravitate towards the kitchen, where everybody feels most comfortable and no one cares about the tell-tale signs of making ends meet. It is also the place where much of the traditional "women's work" is carried out. Several poems in this section develop the idea presented in "Collage in Brown" that the working-class Chicana who wants to write must do so whenever she can, since for economic reasons she must work to survive and has little or no leisure time to devote to writing. In the first section, a quote from "Speaking in Tongues" had presented the Chicana's perspective on Virginia Woolf's famous advice to women writers: "Forget the room of one's own—write in the kitchen, lock yourself up in the bathroom. Write on the bus or the welfare line, on the job or during meals, between sleeping or waking. . . . While you wash the floor or clothes listen to the words chanting in your body."

The section is permeated by the idea of redefining the roles traditionally assigned to women, according to their own inner needs and vision of themselves. "Plática de sobremesa" opens with a poem which functions as a prologue, recited by the chorus of all four actresses. "Dejo de llamarle árbol al árbol" by Genoveva Chacón[12] is an intensely lyrical expression of the desire to shed fixed identities and roles, to penetrate with the transforming power of poetry through the names to the essence of things: "Dejo de llamarle árbol al árbol / porque no es más que el ala de un pájaro en vuelo / que nos cubre del fuego." Following the advice given in "Collage in Brown," a woman sits at the kitchen table writing, though the poem she recites, "Afirmación culinaria" by Miriam Bornstein-Somoza,[13] reveals that domestic duties may suffer in the process: "Se me han quemado los frijoles / por vivir / en un no sé qué mundo de versos / . . . por pensar y sentir / un mundo que existe, / . . . en el aire / agua / fuego tierra / y unas cuantas líneas de un poema." A woman and her father (played by one of the actresses) approach the table and sit facing each other. The writer witnesses their conversation, a piece called "Amor y libertad" by Rosa M. Carrillo, in which the daughter stands up to the father's objections to her living away from home to study and work. The piece captures the pain involved in the clash between traditional family values and the Chicana's changing self-image and desire for independence. When the father reproaches her and her sister for not caring enough about their parents, the Chicana replies angrily: "Ay, Daddy. Ya he lavado, planchado y limpiado por tres años. ¿Qué más quieres?"

These words are followed by a blackout. The lights go up on three women pantomiming household tasks. The fragments they recite from "Patchwork" by Lucha Corpi, begin with a close relationship between the task and the poetic image, recalling Anzaldúa's admonition to use such menial tasks as a trampoline to lyrical expression ("Mientras plancho / una voz adentro / me avisa: / 'El alma necesita / arrugas / necesita pliegues / alforzas y otros / motivos de edad"), but gradually become more abstract in inspiration: "Love / I am full of thorns / full of petals / I carry the complicated / simplicity / of the word / between breast / and backbone." Although a blackout occurs after these lines, when the lights come up the technique of addressing a lover is continued in "Josie Bliss" by Sandra Cisneros.[15]

The previous poems affirmed the unfathomable essence and limitless transformations of the self; in "Josie Bliss" the woman extends the same privacy of multiplicity to her male partner. She contemplates him in sleep, wondering about the parts of his self that are closed to her: "this tiger circle / this knife blade / man I have no power over." As if to remind her of the positive aspects of the boundless facets of her own self and the search for new identities, an "echo" repeats four lines from the prologue: "Y dejo de llamarme a mí misma por mi nombre / porque soy más piedra quieta en el camino / en un camino que corre y se cuelga en un puente sobre el mar." The section closes with a choral recitation of "when all the yous" in its entirety, providing a comment on the previous poems, which have confronted the difficult task of writing about women's changing reality and sharing their vision with other women: "when all the yous / of my poetry / were really / she or her / and i could never / no / i would never write them / because / of some fears / i never even wanted / to see. / how could i have been frightened / of sharing / the being / and me."[16]

The first three sections explore the necessity to write, the significance of the past and the Chicana's changing self-image. The play peaks in the fourth section, "Tongues of Fire." The fact that this section takes its title from the play itself underlines the importance of its theme, already presented in the quote from "Speaking in Tongues" in "Collage in Brown." The Chicana writer rejects the advice of white men on how *not* to write if they want to "make it," by cultivating an authentic voice which springs from her own particular experience of her sex, her race, her class, her history and her culture. This section makes clear that an essential component of this authentic voice is speaking with "tongues of fire." In her defiant self-definition, the Chicana writer commits herself to the denunciation of injustice, the injustice of social and economic oppression as well as the unjust imposition of sexual stereotypes.

The backbone of this section is a long prose piece called "I'm Talking for Justice" by María Moreno, [17] a farmworker mother of twelve and organizer for the Agricultural Workers' Organizing Committee (AFL-CIO) from 1960 to 1962 in the Fresno area. The piece is a transcription of a talk delivered by the then forty-year-old Moreno, who had the reputation of being a forceful speaker, at a meeting in Berkeley in January 1961 to raise funds for lettuce workers of Imperial County who were striking for $1.25 an hour. Carolina Juárez' delivery of this moving speech documenting the exploitation of farmworkers and the hardships they endure was one of the highlights of the show. In her dignity, her articulate honesty and determination to fight to change the lives of farmworkers for the better, María Moreno represents the tradition of strength, endurance and fighting spirit that Chicana writers celebrate and affirm as their own.

The narrative of "I'm Talking for Justice" was broken at two points by two poems. The first, "Napa, California" by Ana Castillo,[18] also dealt with the theme of farmwork, giving poetic expression to what María Moreno attested to in her autobiographical statement. Two women pantomimed farmwork and spoke the lines of the dialogue forming the center of the poem ("bueno pues ¿qué vamos a hacer, Ambrosia? / bueno pues ¡seguirle, comadre, seguirle!"), while the actress who recited the rest of the text stood to one side. The poem captures the endless cycle of back-breaking work which wears their life away: "In fields / so vast / that our youth seems / to pass before us / and we have grown / very / very / old / by dark / . . . while the end / of each day only brings / a tired night / that waits for the sun / and the land / that in turn waits / for us."

The second poem, "Our Side of It" by Marina Rivera, initiates the series of texts which present an aggressive challenge to stereotyped sex roles. This poem exploits the parallel traditionally established between cats and women, manipulating the negative image of cats to women's advantage by playing with the fear they inspire because of their mysteriousness and their association with witches. Amid "jests of nine lives" cats are drowned in rivers and abandoned on freeways. The poetic voice explodes the myth ("Truth is our bodies / make a smudge of blood / a furred clump / on the freeway / just as dead / as the next mongrel") and suggests that the real reason for the fearful prejudice against cats is their despised independence: "that we licked our / own backs / instead of their hands / that we mocked their gates / vaulted their fences." The theme of fear also appears at the conclusion of María Moreno's speech: "What I say is truth, and I'm not afraid to say it. For too long the agricultural worker's been afraid. When somebody hollers, we jump. We never answer back. Well, I'm not afraid no more." "Collage in Brown," in one of the quotes from Anzaldúa's "Speaking in Tongues," had already introduced the theme of fear, associated with the empowering act of writing, of speaking out: "Writing is dangerous, because we are afraid of what the writing reveals: the fears, the angers, the strengths of a woman under the triple or quadruple oppression. Yet in that very act lies our survival because a woman who writes has power. And a woman with power is feared."

Like "Our Side of It," the poem which follows Moreno's monologue, "El diablo en forma de mujer" as told by Juana Esquer,[19] plays with the fear of women expressed in certain negative stereotypes. While "Our Side of It" is subtle, tongue-in-cheek, metaphorical and ironic, "El diablo" exemplifies the broad farcical humor of the oral tradition, in this case, of Texan folklore. The piece, which dramatizes the misogynic belief that women are the instruments of the devil, was presented as a small play-within-the-play. One actress recited Juana's narrative, telling how her uncle, after one too many at the *cantina*, pursues a woman with loose hair and seductive gait that appears before him. When he finally catches up to her in an abandoned house, she turns to reveal the face of the devil. Two women played the parts of the woman and the uncle. The actress delivered the uncle's lines in an exaggerated slapstick style which inspired a great deal of laughter in the audience.

The two short poems which followed the little skit continued the task of destroying stereotyped attitudes towards women through humor. "In a Red-Neck Bar down the Street" by Sandra Cisneros shatters the myth of "feminine" behavior. The poem captures the consternation of the men in the bar caused by the narrator's friend Pat's ability to chug down a bottle of Pabst held in her teeth in one swig, "glugging like a watercooler." With obvious enjoyment, the narrator points out how this "crazy" behavior is viewed as somehow trespassing on forbidden territory: "boy that crazy / act every time gets them / bartender runs over / says lady don't / do that again." Lorna Dee Cervantes' well-known "You cramp my style, baby"[20] is a hilariously searing indictment of the Chicano Movement male whose enthusiastic embrace of "La Raza" and Chicano culture includes the perpetuation of stereotyped sex roles for Chicanas.

"Tongues of Fire" closes on a softer note with "When We Are Able" by Bernice Zamora,[21] combining the awareness of social injustice with the theme of male/female relationships. The poem addresses the impact of poverty and oppression on personal lives and the difficulty of finding happiness in such a world: "when we move from this colony / of charred huts that surround / our grey, wooden, one-roomed house, / we will marry, querido, / we will marry." The intimate tone of the poem is heightened by soothing repetitions. The "when . . . / we will marry . . ." construction is repeated three times, the last instance containing an internal rhythm of three as well: "when you are able to walk / without trembling, / smile / without crying, / and eat without fear, / we will marry, querido, / we will marry." The delivery of this poem demonstrated how successfully choral poetry can bring out the structure and meaning of a poetic text. The first two stanzas, ending with the refrain, were recited by two different actresses. The first part of the final tripart stanza was divided among three voices and all joined in chorus to pronounce the final refrain.

The fifth section of *Tongues of Fire*, "Visions," gathers together the main themes of the previous sections and culminates the show with an expansion of consciousness unprecedented in the depiction of the Chicana in Chicano theater. The final section expresses her thirst for knowledge, for immortality, the search for a voice with which to express her far-reaching visions. "Visions" opens with lines from "Orgánico" by Emy López already quoted in "Collage in Brown" ("quedará / de mí / únicamente / un poema") which will function as the structural and thematic link between the poems of this section. The initial quote leads directly into the core text of "Voices," Lorna Dee Cervantes' poem "Visions of Mexico While at a Writing Symposium in Port Townsend, Washington," key segments of which had already been heard in "Collage in Brown." The poem was delivered uninterrupted by many interpolated texts, divided among three actresses; another recited the hard-hitting quote heading the poem which condenses the dilemma and goal of the Chicana writer: "This world understands nothing but words and you have come into it with almost none." In order to speak out against social injustice, to document the true historical experience of her illiterate ancestors and to dispel stereotyped misunderstandings about her people, the Chicano writer must conquer the word which has been denied her by the same unjust society:

> there are songs in my head I could sing you
> songs that could drone away
> all the mariachi bands you thought you ever heard
> songs that could tell you what I know
> or have learned from my people
> but for that   I need words
> simple black nymphs between white sheets of paper
> obedient words   obligatory words   words I steal
> in the dark when no one can hear me.

This poem returns to the theme of the crucial relationship between history and poetry: the importance of the past in the present and the role of the poem as a poetic document for the future. The lines from "Orgánico" are recited here to remind us of "what is left behind": the poem.

The following text, "Bloodline" by Alma Villanueva,[22] makes it clear that something else besides poetry is left behind to form a new heritage for the future. "Bloodline" celebrates the relationship between mother and daughter, reaffirming the links between women through time brought out in "The Past within Us" but concentrating on the future: "as / you grow old with me, I / grow young with / you—blooming, / bleeding from the / same, sturdy bush, / my daughter."

"Orgánico" reappears here, but continues past the first lines to its conclusion: "se sentirá / solamente / el aroma de un cementerio / y / en mi lecho de huesos / rondarán los lamentos / de gusanos / en fiesta / sobreviviendo." This meditation on survival and death is followed by the last poem of the show, "Memoria total" by Lucha Corpi, which confronts the mystery of death with the desire for transcendence, the quest for universal knowledge:

> One day I'll wake up
> and I'll have forgotten everything
> My eyes will search the whiteness

not realizing that they themselves are snow
I'll be everywhere
because I'll be nowhere
with all the time between my hands
and no more space
than what hangs suspended
between death and oblivion
Then I'll know everything
Entonces lo sabré todo

This striving to know everything and the urgent need to express that knowledge and pass it along to others lies at the heart of *Tongues of Fire*. Only after experiencing the entire show is the meaning of the saying on the title page illuminated in relationship to what the play means: "El árbol por su fruto se conoce." On one level, the "fruit" by which the tree is known is the poetry "left behind" by the Chicana writer which expresses a specific historical experience as women and as Chicanas. On another level, the "fruit" is the daughter, ourselves as the daughters of our mothers, our mothers as the daughters of our grandmothers, our own daughters and by extension, the connections that exist among a community of women in a particular time and through the continuum of history.

Tongues of Fire is both the successful dramatization of the obstacles which the Chicana writer must overcome to accomplish her goals and a tribute to the individual women who have expressed their struggles, dreams and visions in their poetry. Although the poems stand on their own, existing independently as poetic texts, *Tongues of Fire* is much more than an anthology of Chicana poetry. It is the particular thematic development and artistic arrangement of poems, prose pieces, and quotes from "Speaking in Tongues" which make *Tongues of Fire* a text in its own right with a cluster of specific meanings to impart. With the script as a basis, Brinson-Pineda, Curiel and the ensemble as a whole created a memorable theatrical experience which presented coherently and powerfully a certain statement about Chicanas and the importance of writing.

In its organizational aspect, *Tongues of Fire* exemplifies an alternative strategy. In the history of the Chicano theater movement, the most popular model for doing theater has involved working with an already existing teatro or founding a new one, as in the case of Valentina and the new groups springing up in the Bay Area. Yet the overall number of Chicano teatros is shrinking due to the combined onslaught of organizational, economic and personal problems. Valentina's own trajectory illustrates how difficult it is to survive as an institutionalized entity. Very few people continue to work full time in teatro, subsisting on meager salaries and struggling constantly for the economic survival of the group, while part-time theater work involves other difficulties. Personal relationships, full-time jobs and child care are factors which severely limit the time available to work on teatro.

Tongues of Fire represents a possible model which calls for the temporary pooling and concentration of energies on a specific project of limited duration. For the realization of such a theatrical event, the organizers can draw on experienced theater workers and writers in their area. Ideally, this project could be carried out within the context of economic support, such as the funded Chicana conference which allowed for monetary compensation of actresses, director, script writer and lighting technician. After a limited number of performances, the group would simply disband, having contributed to the development of Chicano theater and avoiding the protracted problems of a permanent company.

That this may be a viable path is suggested by *Tongues of Fire* and also by the production of the play *The Reunion*, performed in the Mission Cultural Center late in Summer of 1981. *The Reunion* by Edgar Poma was mounted by a group called Teatro Yerbabuena, composed of members of Teatro Latino and Teatro Gusto who came together to work on the controversial topic of homosexuality in the context of the Chicano family. The play was well received and stimulated discussion on this important issue within the community.

The show put together by the temporary group could always be resurrected and rehearsed for additional performances by the same group or by a new group; the same people could regroup to work on a new project or disperse to work with new people. The possibilities are many, but the essential idea is one of temporary banding and disbanding of individuals from a pool of committed, experienced theater workers.

While the advantages of this performance-oriented strategy in which all energies can be concentrated on production are clear, working in a collective over a long period of time is a valuable learning experience in itself. The support provided by the members to one another and the opportunity to put into daily practice the political theories they attempt to dramatize in their plays can be of more lasting value to the individuals involved than the fleeting impact of a performance on a given audience. The "hit-and-run" project may be plagued by the same problems as the permanent teatro: personality conflicts, limited rehearsal time, etc. And with the relatively short time available to smooth over these rough spots, the tensions can show in the performance. What we may want to consider is not so much the superiority of one way of doing theater over the other, but the necessity in these hard times of diversifying our strategies with the goal of exploiting our potential to the maximum.

[1] For an analysis of the 11th Festival, see *La Revista Literaria de El Tecolote*, II/3-4 (December 1981). The entire number was dedicated to a critical review of the Festival by the San Francisco collective Poetasumanos, of which I am also a member. Included are two pieces on women: "The Role of Women in Chicano Theater Organizations" and "The Image of the Chicana in Teatro."

[2] For example, Teatro Raíces, working in the agit-prop tradition of popular political theater, performed a series of *actos* on an open-air platform during the 24th Street Fair. For a discussion of the *acto* form and its evolution through time, see Jorge A. Huerta's *Chicano Theater: Themes and Forms* (Ypsilanti, Michigan: Bilingual Press, 1982).

[3] From an interview with Smiley Rojas.

[4] I would like to thank Barbara Brinson-Pineda for the interview and the script which provided me with indispensable information for the discussion of *Tongues of Fire*.

[5] From my interview with Natalia Ceballos, Eva Chaidez and Cara Hill.

[6] (Watertown, Mass.: Persephone Press, 1981)

[7] III/1 (March 1982).

[8] Published in her book *Emplumada* (Pittsburgh: University of Pittsburgh Press, 1981).

[9] *La Opinión* (19 April 1981), p. 11

[10] The three poems by Lucha Corpi are from her book *Palabras de mediodía / Noon Words*, trans. Catherine Rodríguez-Nieto (Berkeley: El Fuego de Aztlán Publications, 1980).

[11] "Arriaga" was published in *XismeArte*, 7 (January 1981); "María la O" appeared in *Revista Chicano-Riqueña* (I will abbreviate *RCR*), VII/4 (1979).

[12] Published in *Metamorfosis*, III/2 and IV/1 (1980/1981).

[13] Published in her book *Bajo cubierta* (Tucson: Scorpion Press, 1976).

[14] *Second Chicano Literary Prize* (Irvine: Dept. of Spanish and Portuguese, Univ. of California, 1976), pp. 9-16.

[15] *RCR*, VII/3 (1979).

[16] *Festival Flor y Canto* (Los Angeles: University of Southern California, 1976), p. 55.

[17] Published in *Mexican Women in the United States: Struggles Past and Present*, eds. Magdalena Mora and Adelaida R. del Castillo (Los Angeles: Chicano Studies Research Center Publications, Occasional Paper No. 2, 1980). Originally published in *Regeneración*, I/10 (1971).

[18] *RCR*, IV/4 (1976).

[19] In *Mexican Folk Narrative from the Los Angeles Area*, compiled by Elaine K. Miller (Austin: University of Austin Press, 1973).

[20] Published in *El Fuego de Aztlán*, I/4 (1977).

[21] In her book with José Antonio Burciaga, *Restless Serpents* (Menlo Park, Ca.: Diseños Literarios, 1976).

[22] Published in *XismeArte*, 7 (January 1981).

Roberta Orona-Cordova

Zoot Suit and the Pachuco Phenomenon: An Interview with Luis Valdez

Luis Valdez, playwright, poet, director and actor, was born in Delano, California, on June 26, 1940, to migrant farmworker parents. Second of a family of ten brothers and sisters, Valdez followed the crops picking grapes at around age six. It was at this time that his interest in theatre began; however, because of the family's nomadic life—traveling between orchards up and down California—his very first attempt to enter the theatrical world was thwarted. "I was supposed to be in a Christmas program in the first grade but I never played in it because my family moved away before we performed." Valdez never forgot this incident and therefore studied drama at San Jose State College.

Before graduating from San Jose College in 1964, the Drama Department produced his first full-length play, *The Shrunken Head of Pancho Villa*. At the end of 1965 when César Chávez launched his historic Delano Grape Strike, Valdez returned to his birthplace to work as an organizer for the farmworkers union. It was there that he joined his farmworker roots and his theatre background by founding El Teatro Campesino.

In 1967, during the Teatro's first national tour, Valdez and his company began to receive wide attention from publications, including *The New Yorker* and *Newsweek*. In 1968 Teatro was awarded the off-Broadway Obie. Teatro also received the Los Angeles Drama Critics Circle Award in 1969 and 1971. In 1972 Luis Valdez created for television *Los Vendidos* which later won several awards, among them, the Emmy. In 1976 and 1977, *El Corrido* was on national television (PBS), written by Valdez in collaboration with El Teatro.

In the winter of 1977, motion picture audiences saw him in Universal's *Which Way Is Up?* starring Richard Pryor. Valdez also collaborated on the script with Pryor. Visiting eight western European countries in the fall of 1976, the Teatro's first major European tour featured Valdez as the character of Jesus "Pelado" Rasquache in *La Carpa*.

Luis Valdez has emerged as an international leader in alternative theatre. He currently serves on the advisory boards of the International Theatre Institute's American Center, and the PBS network *Visions* series. He was the U.S. representative to the 1971 Third World Theatre Conference held in the Philippines, and a delegate to the First American Congress of Theatre in 1973 at Princeton University. In 1976, he was appointed to the nine-member California Arts Council by Governor Edmund G. Brown, Jr., and was elected to the Board of Directors of the Theatre Communications, to the theatre community of America. Valdez has also taught drama courses at the Universities of California at Berkeley and Santa Cruz and at California State University, Fresno.

In January of 1978, Valdez was named a recipient of the prestigious Rockefeller Foundation Playwright-in-Residence Award in connection with the production of his original play, *Zoot Suit*. He was commissioned to write and direct *Zoot Suit* for production by the Mark Taper Forum of the Center Theatre Group in Los Angeles. After a successful run at the Taper, in August of 1978 the play moved to a nine-month extension of sold-out performances and hit reviews at the Aquarius Theatre in Hollywood, where the movie version of *Zoot Suit* was filmed in 1981.

This interview took place in Luis Valdez's office in the Teatro Campesino's playhouse in San Juan Bautista two weeks after the film version of *Zoot Suit* opened in New York City in January 1982.

Interviewer: Why do you think *Zoot Suit* is an important film today?

Valdez: Well, there probably isn't a filmmaker alive that doesn't think that his film is important. So, whatever I have to say about *Zoot Suit* has to be qualified with that. I'm speaking about my product and so if it hadn't been important to me, I wouldn't have done it. It's important for a number of different reasons. For one, it's the first film within the Hollywood structure that is conceived, written and directed by a Chicano, with a certain amount of artistic control, which was part of the deal to begin with. And if you knew how many deals go down in Hollywood and never get beyond the lunch stage, you'd know how any film that gets made in Hollywood has certain importance, just by virtue of the fact that it got made. This particular film had a lot going against it after New York and there were a lot of conditions that were slapped on it because of the criticial response in New York City.

Interviewer: Were these conditions made by people in the movie industry?

Valdez: Absolutely. There was a lot of interest going into New York after Hollywood. There were a lot of offers, including offers of money, which I refused because I was always interested in artistic control.

None of the studios or producers would consider my directing a movie, for one.

Interviewer: Can you elaborate on this a bit more?

Valdez: Well, I was a first-time director. I had never directed a film for one; and that was basically it. I suppose there were other reasons; I was a Chicano on top of everything else. And I had difficulties even getting guarantees that I would be able to do the screenplay. Basically, what they wanted was the idea. They wanted the title, *Zoot Suit*. They wanted the notoriety of the play in Los Angeles, and they wanted to convert it into their own film. The concepts that we were kicking around at the time were very different from those in the final film. The crucial element was the character of the Pachuco. That was always the first question that came up: "What are you going to do with the Pachuco?" Originally, the film was conceived in a lot of these discussions with a very different concept in mind; it was more historically based, more realistic, more observing of the Pachuco phenomenon from the outside, rather than from the inside, sort of a broad panorama of the times. While these discussions were going on, Steven Speilberg's movie, *1941*, was just getting into production. Everybody in Hollywood had heard that he was going to do the zoot suit riots as a part of his film. I think the original script had a much larger section on the zoot suit riots than that which actually appeared in the final film. But that news automatically began to change our discussions because somebody was already doing a film on the zoot suit riots, and Speilberg, no less. So in these discussions we began considering other approaches in terms of style and treatment, until we got to New York, where we were assassinated by the critics. All serious negotiations for the play came to a halt. It's very important that people consider the fate of *Zoot Suit* in New York City both as play and film, because the movie critics also slit our throats in New York. It was no different than what they did to the play. It comes from an entrenched racist attitude that has been there for as long as the westward movement has existed, which is well over a hundred years. This attitude refuses to allow us at this time to penetrate on our own terms. It will not allow blacks to penetrate on their own terms either. It does not want us to penetrate into Broadway or penetrate into the closed circle of New York literary publications. It does not want any genuine voice from the West Coast to break through, much less a non-white, Chicano-Indian viewpoint.

Interviewer: Is there any other reason why the film was criticized so severely?

Valdez: Part of the problem was the fact that I chose to maintain the Pachuco, and certain attitudes about American society in general.

I was asked to give up the Pachuco and a certain kind of attitude and maybe acceptance would be forthcoming.

Interviewer: And you wouldn't?

Valdez: And I won't.

Interviewer: Would that be a compromise for you?

Valdez: Yes, that would be a compromise; it would be to wash down the drain everything that the work is intended to do, which is to break through on our own terms.

Interviewer: What is it about the Pachuco attitude that is offensive or that they wanted you to eliminate?

Valdez: He is the rebel. The recalcitrant rebel who refuses to give in, who refuses to bend, refuses to admit that he is wrong. He is incorrigible. And the way that the Pachucho appears in the film and in the play makes a very strong statement. The stance is almost ideological, even cultural; it's mythical. They know then, the Anglo critics, almost instinctively, even if they don't bother to think it out, that what this figure represents is a self-determined identity; it comes from its own base. That's been my argument all along through my work; that we have our own fundamental base from which to work. It's very strong and it's the foundation of civilization; it's not just a by-product of everything that is happening. All of these things are implicit in *Zoot Suit*, but very few critics have actually penetrated into the real meaning of the play. The more negative the critics, the more reluctant and unwilling they are to discuss it, so all they can do is just kick at it; all they can do is say that it is dumb, that it's sophomoric. Reviews, of course, on the west coast have been totally different, so there is a real dichotomy between the way the film was generally received by critics on the east coast and on the west coast.

Interviewer: Do you think the Pachuco is right in what he believes, what he represents in his attitude, his rebelliousness?

Valdez: It depends on what you feel he represents. It requires an interpretation because the Pachuco is neither good nor bad, he is both. He is, if anything, an abstract person who, in the mind of Henry Reyna, is aiding Henry to achieve a higher level of consciousness. I choose to call it the *internal authority*. I mean it has been described a number of different ways; anything from religious terms to psychological terms. You can take your pick. I like to use the word myth, and a lot of people, I suppose, don't really understand what the old use of the word used to be, because myth refers to an underlying structure of a truth that is just below the surface of reality. You could say that the atom is a myth. Nobody's ever seen one so you sort of have to believe it because it is just a structure.

Interviewer: What is this "entrenched attitude" that won't allow Chicanos to penetrate the literary and film industries?

Valdez: This attitude I refer to is the white man's sense of arrogance and belief that the truth resides in Western European culture, and that whether you are talking about capitalism or communism, or about Protestantism or Catholicism, only *their* science, *their* religion, *their* politics and *their* arts are sophisticated enough to be valid. Naturally, the entire non-white world from Africa to Asia has been victimized and colonized by this incredibly arrogant attitude, but it is in America that this ignorance has come to roost. Here, a transplanted European culture is masquerading as American culture, and the way of life of the real natives has been distorted, stolen, ignored or forgotten. Chicanos, any way you cut it, are native Americans. Of course, all of us that are Chicanos can also relate to the Hispanic part of our culture, and we should. But then there is the other, the ignored part, the despised part, the dehumanized part, which is the *indígena*. And it seems to me that part cannot be ignored forever. It was, again speaking very relatively, too effective in its time. You have only to draw a line across the centuries, in terms of achievements of other cultures, to know that pre-Columbian culture was highly civilized. Here in America, speaking again in terms of the cultural patterns of the continent as a whole, there was a map, and that map is being ignored. And that map had a hub, and that hub was in Mexico. We are the New World. You cannot dismiss as much civilization as Mexico has had, especially if you know anything about it. It is an ancient pride that makes us rebel, that makes it ultimately inconceivable to us that all that culture must be lost, that all the truth, power and goodness in life resides in assimilation into the Anglo-American mode. You have only to make the simplest kind of historical and cultural analysis to know that there is something about pre-Colombian civilization that cannot be ignored or dismissed. Consequently, your average Anglo in the street will eventually come around so that he's spouting a new 21st-century "spiritually scientific" philosophy that is very close to the *indio* philosophy of our Mayan and Toltec ancestors, and then all those Chicanos that are following the white man will come around to their own culture; but only by virtue of following the white man. But the white man cannot see us as clearly as we see ourselves. You cannot take a reality like *pachuquismo* and say Pachucos are what they are, just on the basis of what they look like to the white man. The real significance of El Pachuco in *Zoot Suit* is deeper than most people realize. Anytime that a new identity is created, it emerges as a power that is raw, terrible and disgusting to some, and glorious to others. Nobody knows, for instance, what Jesus Christ ultimately looked like. If he appeared before a lot of people today, they would dismiss him as some kind of tramp. And other people would be able to see the glow, you see. This is the way it is; individuals or those things that change reality sometimes come through life with frightening power. Revolutionaries are very frightening, prophets are frightening; people that have a certain kind of hidden power scare other people. They are intimidating; there was a lot of that in the Pachuco. But those in the know cannot fail to recognize him (in the film) as a reincarnation of the ancient god Tezcatlipoca. His style, his colors, his powers are all attributes of ancient wisdom: "la tinta negra y roja" of the lord of education, the dean of the school of hard knocks. El Pachuco is thus a symbol of our identity, our total identity, with ancient roots.

Interviewer: What is the relationship between the Pachuco and Henry? Is the Pachuco Henry's consciousness?

Valdez: As I said, I call the Pachuco the internal authority. I know he's been called "conscience," he's been called alter-ego, but he is not so much alter-ego as he is super-ego—using Freudian terms—because super-ego is your conscience that tells you what's right and what's wrong. Again, how does the super-ego function in our lives? How does this internal authority appear in our lives? He doesn't really appear as a person, of course. But he sometimes appears as our own voice, talking to us inside our own heads. You know the old cartoons we used to see, the conscience appeared as the little halo around or over the head. And then there was the *diablo*, the little devil, and actually the super-ego is both: the devil and the angel, not one or the other. And your conscience is both, and your conscience plays with you, it tempts you, it challenges you, it presents you with alternatives and lets you decide. It goads you.

Interviewer: What does the Pachuco do?

Valdez: All those things with Henry, good and bad, depending on what your point of view is. Some of the things you agree with, some of the things, you don't. You have people agreeing with different aspects of the Pachuco. Some people like him, some people don't and can't stand him. Some people feel he is evil, and some people feel that he is basically good. It depends on who you talk to. Some people feel he is a monster and some people feel that he is a hero, that he is a figure to emulate.

Interviewer: He seems aware of Henry's reality. The Pachuco is wise.

Valdez: It's not only that; he's super human. He's running the show and for once, from a storytelling point of view, I wanted a Chicano in control of the story, and so the Pachuco is the editor. He is the one that snaps it on and snaps it off. He is the one that controls the point of view, if you will. That's very important, the fact that it's being seen through this point of view. That became a real question, a literal question when we got down to planning our shots, or even when I started writing the screenplay, because point of view is the most essential question you could ask about any screenplay. What's the eye, who is looking at this? Ultimately what you are left with is one camera lens and you are looking at limited space, the limited shot, the limited angle, and you have to ask yourself, "Okay, who's eye is this?" Henry's story is being observed by the Pachuco most of the time, but occasionally you get Henry's point of view of the Pachuco, and that's the crux of the story. It's obviously Henry's struggle with himself. It is Henry's struggle with himself on three planes, and the physical is not nearly as physicalized in *Zoot Suit*, the film, as it might have been. But it's certainly emotional, and it's certainly intellectual. It's the intellectual part that is unexpected and unappreciated and unwanted by a lot of the general public. You don't often get intellectual movies, which get into discussions, but that is something that was very natural in the play. Since we transferred the play, it just had to be. I didn't want to present an unthinking character. Henry Reyna thinks and has a dialogue going with himself, the way we all do. The way Pachucos even do. And we are portrayed on the screen as being thoughtless, so I also wanted to utilize the device of the Pachuco to show the mental processes inside the head of Henry Reyna, and deliberately so.

Interviewer: What was this struggle like within the consciousness of the Pachuco in the '40s?

Valdez: It was a struggle for identity, because an identity was needed. The question is, of course, why not assimilate when it could be so convenient? Well, for one, the society won't allow many of us to assimilate. We just can't pass for white, whether we want to or not. And the other is, what are we assimilating into? That question must always be asked. There are a whole lot of questions and a whole lot of answers that require a certain amount of discussion. But let me say it's natural for people to confuse the Pachuco in the movie with their experiences of Pachuquismo. All I can say is that in my case, in my life experience, the Pachucos were both good and bad, exactly as I represent them, because the Pachucos that I knew were bad guys, but at the same time it seemed to me they were saying some rather important things and making rather important statements. They were standing up to a society that was, for me as a kid, obviously unjust, obviously racist, and it seemed to me that they had some balls. I admired that. They were the only ones that were doing it. Everybody else, as far as I could see, was holding their hat in their hands. The Pachucos were not afraid. They were dealing with an oppressive inferiority complex. It seemed that the Americano had everything, that the Gringo was everything, and that the Mexicano was nothing. But there were always fights in the barrio—people taking out their own frustration on themselves. There was a lot of drunkenness and a lot of poverty and lot of hard work, and for what? Along come these Pachucos and they dress good and look nice, and they stand out. Yes they do get busted and jailed and they are obscene and dangerous and drug addicts, but that still does not cancel out some of the positive qualities, as far as my experience was concerned. Now it so happens, later on in the '50s I got stopped occasionally by the Pachucos for carrying too many books home, but I was always able to talk my way out of it; and I learned a bit of *caló*. I learned not to divorce myself from those basic elements in the barrio. No matter what I wanted to do, I knew that I needed them and they needed me. That's always been a principle of mine: not to divorce myself from any of the elements of my reality, no matter how unattractive they may seem. I have tried to resist the bourgeois temptation to look down my nose at the lower class *rasquaches* because, you know, I'm a lower class *rasquache*. If it hadn't been for my interest in the arts, I probably would have ended up in the joint somewhere; but I had something to do.

Interviewer: What would you say to a Chicano who asks you why you glorified the Pachuco? He is an attractive person, a very attractive person.

Valdez: I would say I haven't glorified him. I've presented him both as good and bad. There are a lot of negative things about the Pachuco, and I make no bones about it.

Interviewer: Can you explain this a little more?

Valdez: Sure. I mean, as the character in the film, El Pachuco is always getting in the way of things that Henry's trying to do: his relationship with Della for one, his relationship with Alice, another, and his relationship with his family. There are things that Henry's trying not to do, but the Pachuco is goading him. He goads him into getting into that last fight which gets him into trouble. By the same token, the Pachuco is also goading Henry into a greater level of self-consciousness. I think what you have to ask is what does the Pachuco represent? At the same time that he represents those real life Pachucos, he represents the essence of what Pachuquismo is all about, which is this struggle for identity.

Interviewer: You have discussed Pachuquismo in terms of a struggle for identity, maturity and the struggle toward consciousness. Can you elaborate on this latter point?

Valdez: Well, we have to be as conscious as we can in life, it seems to me. I mean that's the life process. You live, you're born and you become conscious of your surroundings, and other people and yourself, and that process continues until the day you die. And depending on your level of consciousness, you will do one thing or the other. It seems to me a whole argument could be made that the whole world is into a struggle with consciousness. That's the struggle of everything. That's the underlying force in nature: the struggle towards consciousness, towards awareness. The Pachuco phenomenon was part of this process and part of the struggle. As it is, it helps the rest of us who never became Pachucos, who never could be Pachucos, to become more aware of ourselves. Now consciousness, an awareness doesn't always develop one way or another. You really have to consider where the person is in life, and I don't think that any of these Pachucos would have necessarily become idealogues, because there was no college education. Later on some of these Pachucos, through different methods, were able to get to school, or maybe they just educated themselves in the *pinta*. Then they were able to trust themselves in ideological fashion, but intelligence manifested itself in a number of different ways. I think that this country's pursuit of wealth is adolescent; its underlying motive in capitalist society is to get wealth. To acquire wealth is the key to power and happiness. This is basically an adolescent solution to life, and while we persist as a society now, as a world, as we persist in looking for that solution, we are going to get the other one, which is the adolescent need for heroism and war. So it's not surprising that this country has gone through a roller coaster of wars and depressions that relate directly to inflation, unemployment, depression, military engagements, then prosperity, then peace, and more inflation and unemployment. I mean it's just up and down, up and down, and that's the history of the United States; but that's because it's adolescent. It's an adolescent world. The way people kill themselves off, it's an adolescent world. I sometimes get the impression the whole earth is nothing but a kindergarten, grammar and high school.

Interviewer: Do you think the phenomenon of Pachuquismo is an adolescent phenomenon?

Valdez: Yes, but there is more to Pachuquismo than meets the eye. It has something to do with maturity, and it has something to do with a heroic attitude for life.

Interviewer: How did the Pachuco experience influence Chicanos?

Valdez: The Pachuco phenomenon gave every urban Chicano after that the ability to be urban. It gave us an urban identity that we never had before. I mean, who were these Pachucos? They were the sons of campesinos that had fled Mexico, and these campesinos had never had a chance to live in cities and it was too late for them to really wrestle with the basic problems of what it meant to live in an

Anglo society. Their children grew up in the streets of some of these southwestern towns and cities. They had to deal with it because it was their life and they had to deal with being urban and the way that they dealt with it is they invented Pachuquismo. They took on the zoot suit; they took on the Pachuco slang and they developed a mode of life. Since then, of course, the life style branched out and one piece became the low rider movement and another piece became drugs, but some of those pieces became leaders like César Chávez, who was a Pachuco. Other Pachucos became teachers. It's like a seed that opens up and you have a lot of branches; a plant that grows out of the seed.

Interviewer: There are several lines in the movie which give the audience insight into the conflict Henry Reyna experiences in his relationship with the Pachuco: his *internal authority*. Can you interpret those for us?

Valdez: Sure. Which ones?

Interviewer: "Don't hate your *Raza* more than you love the Gringo."

Valdez: Well, you remember that appears in the Saturday night dance sequence, where Rafas and Henry get into a knife fight. What happens just before this is that Rafas asks Henry to gang up on the sailor. Henry looks at the sailor and says "I don't like the odds." Rafas says, "You think you're some hot shit just because the Navy accepted you," and then Henry says, "As if you didn't try." The knife fight begins and Henry gets really pissed at Rafas and he's about to cut him up. That's when the Pachuco stops him and says, "Don't hate your Raza more than you love the Gringo." He's telling Henry to control himself.

Interviewer: Do you mean he loves the Gringo as well?

Valdez: Sure. Well, I mean he's got Anglos in his gang. Later on in the cell, the Pachuco says, "Underneath the big tough bullshit exterior is a little snotnose Mexican kid, begging for the Gringos' attention." A lot of that comes from what was happening forty years ago, along with the whole *Zoot Suit* phenomenon. It seemed to me a lot of those kids were just trying to be Americans.

Interviewer: Are you saying he tried to break away from Pachuquismo and win acceptance by going into the Navy, and never made it?

Valdez: Never made it. The point really of that statement is that you can't really love the Gringo without loving your own people. Unfortunately we still see a lot of people that court the Gringo and go after the Gringo, and they can't do the same thing with their Raza out of some failure in themselves to be able to deal with who they are and accept that.

Interviewer: At the end of the trial Henry stood up to hear the verdict and the sentencing. His stance then was that of a hero, a proud hero, and the Pachuco says, "The barrio needs you, ése, stand up to them in style." What was your intention here?

Valdez: Show the world Hank Reyna has some balls, and remember, "Pachuco yo." It's the rebellion, the defiance, it's stoicism against the obvious injustice. We had already established that in the script. So what do you do in the face of obvious injustice, but stand up and take it, and go on to the next thing.

Interviewer: There is another line which is very poetic. "You're a marijuana dreamer floating in an endless night of unfulfilled fantasies." What are these unfulfilled fantasies?

Valdez: The bottom line of reality: the fact that out of this endless night of unfulfilled fantasies, come fantasies that become real; and that we are all like marijuana dreamers floating in reality. Shakespeare said it differently and better. He said, "We are such stuff as dreams are made on, and our little life is rounded with a sleep." Obviously, I lend a lot of credence to the mind and consciousness. What that does is that it unlocks you from the prison of an overly material universe, and gives you freedom. The material facts of Pachuquismo, for example, are not impressive; that is, the outward view, the external view. Just like the material facts of the poverty of *la raza* are not impressive. We live in a very materialistic society, with a spiritual base that doesn't work. But there are things in life that are not visible, that are nevertheless real. It's like the atom. There are forces that function in life that have to be registered in a different way, other than seeing material measurement. And because they are invisible, many of these phenomena are subject to all kinds of charlatanism, but their reality is nevertheless the substance of art and poetry, not to speak of advanced physics. So why the stuff of dreams, why invoke that, why is Henry Reyna a marijuana dreamer floating in an endless night of unfulfilled fantasies? Because that's where his ultimate power lies. That's where his ultimate humanity lies. It is his cosmic root, and it doesn't mean he doesn't have to deal with the material conditions of his life. He does, as we all do, but it also means that his potential is rooted in infinity. People that root their potential in some kind of limited material manifestation just end up committing suicide.

Interviewer: In one form or another.

Valdez: Yes, in one form or another.

Interviewer: What about, "You know what's wrong with you? You can't stand yourself and you can't stand me telling you." What is it about himself that he can't stand?

Valdez: Well, he had just been rejected by Alice. I mean Alice reaches out and tries to be a friend. And Henry takes it farther and he starts getting romantically involved. So Alice has to backtrack, so Henry then backtracks even more. He goes back to being pissed. He gets pissed at himself and so then the Pachuco brings it out in him.

Interviewer: Why do you think he gets angry at himself?

Valdez: For sticking his neck out, and for thinking that she would accept him.

Interviewer: Did the "real" Henry Reyna fall in love with Alice?

Valdez: Yes. I had to make a choice whether to develop it or not. It took a while to shape it. If you remember, that element was a little bit different in the play. As much as I think Chicanos got off on it, Anglos resented it. They didn't like the romance or the politics of it: a white woman falling in love with a Pachuco. In real life, they fell in love through letters. It was all through letters. The "real" Alice told me she kept them for a long time but eventually discarded them. So for the stage version, I fictionalized the letters they wrote to each other and then dramatized them. They became little scenes in the play. But once you physicalize something like that it runs the danger of becoming soap opera. I was never really able to achieve a point of satisfaction with that scene on the stage. I also had the problem of not finding the right actress until I ran into Tyne Daly. I had met Tyne before, but she was doing other things during the run of the play. I'm sorry we didn't take her to New York, because she would have made a hell of a difference.

Interviewer: What is it about Tyne that made a difference in the film version?

Valdez: Subtlety, honesty, real warmth between Tyne as Alice and Daniel as Henry. The difference is that Tyne has worked through, broken through, the racism. She is married to George Sanford Brown. He's a Cuban, actually, but he's black. He's a black actor doing a lot of directing now. He's a very handsome actor. Just a hell of a man. They love each other tremendously. You can really tell it's an intense relationship. And they have worked through this difference. Acting the scene out with Daniel was not a problem for Tyne, who was the fifth woman to play Alice. But she is a hell of an actress to begin with, very powerful, so obviously she brought great skill to the role.

Interviewer: At the end of the film Henry started to break down, after he had been in solitary. He said, "I know who you are, *carnal*. You are the one who got me here." What is his point in this line?

Valdez: It is Henry coming to terms with himself. How do we all come to terms with ourselves? The power to do it resides in ourselves, with what we do, you see. It's not outside. People on the outside cannot make you free, no more than people on the outside can imprison you. People on the outside cannot make you more or less than what you are. You are what you are and you are what you are in confrontation with yourself. You are your own best judge. And in fact, Henry was in prison and in solitary confinement because of choices that he made, for good or for bad, and that is really the beginning of his liberation, of his way out. So long as he kept blaming the exterior, the deeper he was going to be driven into himself. It happens to people that are catatonic. They can't deal with the external conditions of their life, because they can't deal with themselves, so they go into themselves and stay there.

Interviewer: What made Henry change after being in solitary confinement?

Valdez: It happens to a lot of people. Once you are left alone and you have to think it through, you are either going to survive or you are not going to survive. You are going to figure out your problems, or what went wrong, or where you made the right moves, or the wrong moves. You have to have a reason for finding yourself in a tough situation. That's Henry's problem; and he makes it. He makes it because he comes to terms with himself.

Interviewer: In what way does he make it?

Valdez: He makes it in terms of getting free. He was free already before he was released.

Interviewer: Are you saying the resolution was an internal one, within himself?

Valdez: That's right. Also he is able to get to the point where he hopes once again. Because he was hoping during the trial, you know, that he would get off, yet not hoping enough.

Interviewer: A line that was implicit throughout the movie was, "You are my worst enemy, my best friend, you are myself." There also seems to be a resolution within this statement. Is this what you intended?

Valdez: Yeah. That's Henry's consciousness. He finally sees himself again. He is stripped down and he is in the loincloth. Then Henry sees himself, his brother, and then back as the Pachuco; and the Pachuco is presented as *el indio*. All of that resonates, it resonates deeply in Hank and it's supposed to resonate in the audience as well. And when you see the Pachuco again and Henry sees him, I want people to feel that Hank had a greater degree of self-awareness coming out of prison. The Pachuco is in white and then we see the three different endings that Henry sees as well. I mean he sees himself possibly going back to prison, or going off to war, or getting married and settling down, and those three things are part of Henry's consciousness. He is much more aware of himself, he is much more aware he has three choices. All of this, of course, is implied; it's all implicit; it's all symbolic, but it's there.

Interviewer: What did he do?

Valdez: He did one of those three things. Possibly all of them. I am telling the story. I leave that up to the audience to decide.

Interviewer: The Pachucos called themselves Chicanos. In the family scene Henry's father said, "Don't use that word, it means you're trash." Why was "Chicano" considered a negative word?

Valdez: Chicano was a dirty word. It's still a dirty word to a lot of people. It's gotten more accepted because the media uses it, but it's one of those words that came up from the street, that came up from the barrio, and the street wasn't even paved. And a lot of people assumed it came from *chicanería*, chicanery, which means trickery. A lot of people say that Chicanos are really *gente baja*. That they are trash, brown trash. These people don't want to be associated with Chicanos. It's a word of uncertain origin, just like Pachuco, just like zoot suit.

Interviewer: Mexican-American and Mexican parents found it offensive, then?

Valdez: At that time they found it very offensive, of course. Now everybody uses it whether they want to or not, but it is a word we got from the Pachuco experience. We didn't end up calling ourselves Pachucos, we ended up calling ourselves Chicanos. Part of the point that's implicit there is that the Pachuco is responsible for the word Chicano. He's the one that used it.

Interviewer: Can you summarize the Pachuco phenomenon or Henry Reyna's experience in terms of who he is in relationship to his surroundings, the larger society?

Valdez: Sure. He is the law of contradiction. Some people call him the law of contradiction. Some people call him duality, dialectical materialism. The internal authority that is at work is necessary in the psychological process of individuation that we all undergo. Every one of us, as human beings, undergoes a process whereby we define ourselves as individuals in life. We do it according to our own personal struggles. The whole Sleepy Lagoon case is told in *Zoot Suit* in terms of the personal struggle of Henry Reyna. There isn't a single social event that in some way you cannot define in personal terms, in the personal terms of the individual involved, because there is always an inside personal life, and an external social life in any event. The entire 1960s, for instance, indicates a lot of us were basically changing. We were undergoing change through that period in life, and so it was a very natural union of the external and the internal; the youth and the rebellion and the joy that we felt in our internal personal lives as people that were undergoing their youth. Our young adulthood was reflected in the excitement and the rebellion in the outside world, and so forth. Well, in Henry's case, in 1942, it was a crucial time that involved a lot of young men going off to war and becoming warriors and there was the zoot suit phenomenon which was a uniform of a different kind. So society's battles—both abroad and at home, with its own social levels of racism and economic discrimination—were outside, external reflections of Henry's own internal struggle to deal with his evolving manhood, going from adolescent to young man. This internal struggle was one way to deal with this broad panorama of the Sleepy Lagoon Case. The only way to deal with it was in terms of a person and his struggles to form relationships with people. This is part of what *Zoot Suit* is all about. Let me add that what I have learned from doing this work is that we as Chicanos still have a struggle which needs to be fought, consciously or unconsciously; but the bottom lines have never been so clear to me. Some people don't understand our struggles and so there is a need for a focused, concentrated effort to try and rip through this ignorance.

Interviewer: Octavio Paz in his essay on "The Pachuco and Other Extremes" in *The Labyrinth of Solitude*, 1961, gives his own interpretation of the Pachuco. Can you give us your comments about his interpretation?

Valdez: Sure. What, for instance?

Interviewer: He compares Mexicanos to Pachucos; for example, "We live closed up in ourselves like those taciturn adolescents." Do you feel Pachucos lived closed up within themselves?

Valdez: I think there are always closed human circles. To a certain extent, then, what the Pachucos did is no different than what everybody else does; that is to practice alienation in some sort of organized way. That's what men's secret societies are all about, the Shriners and the Masons. All of those exclusive societies, the country clubs, etc. I mean people naturally form *clicas*, because it makes them feel special. What Octavio Paz is relating is something that is important, but he does not seem to recognize the Pachucos' need to feel special in their own closed circle. What he has stated in *Labyrinth*, if I remember correctly, is that the Pachuco is about as far out as the Mexican can get, or as far in. I mean it is isolation, as far away from normal life as you can get. He saw them as abnormal, as hybrids, sterile and remote. But then you have to ask: "sterile in relation to what?" The very fact that the Pachuco is being considered in the context of Anglo American society changes the point of view. The Pachuco in Los Angeles was confronted with a very different phenomenon, which is Anglo American society, which exists like a wall. Paz was not really in a position to judge the Pachuco or the wall that confronted him. I mean he had some important insights, but he couldn't really get into an understanding of what the Pachuco was without having actually shared some of their experiences by living here. You have to grow up with it, and to be confronted with it on a daily basis. The white society dances around and pretends we are not here. I don't think, at least I assume, that Paz had not known that kind of alienation: to have one's identity totally denied and ignored. The experience of a Mexican going to New York City, having at least Mexico City and a Mexican national identity behind you, is one thing. The experience of a Chicano going to New York is another. It's odd enough to go from East Los Angeles to West Los Angeles and to feel the aliena-tion.

Interviewer: Did you feel that alienation in New York?

Valdez: Yes, and I've gone under the best of conditions. I mean I've done the limousine trip and press conferences and television shows. Yes, I felt the strangeness of it. I might as well have been from Madagascar. I might as well have been from another country. I say this because it's the same frustration the Pachuco felt. I don't think Octavio Paz or any Mexican, unless it is one of those Mexicans that moved and grew up here, really understands that part of the Pachuco experience. The need to stand up and just rebel, to say *no*, is to provide a new possibility: it's to bring a new consciousness into being. Blacks understand it in this country. There is a difference between my point of view and Octavio Paz' even though we may agree on many points. Our conclusions are different.

Interviewer: Will you elaborate on Paz' statement that the Pachuco "flaunts his difference," that he "rejects the society that rejects him?"

Valdez: Right. He flaunts his difference. But what is that difference? Again, where are we coming from? Are we coming from a basic position that takes into account the history of the last 500 years? Not until the pre-Colombian cultures are given their human worth will it be possible to do anything but flaunt this difference. What's interesting is that my experience as a playwright, my experience with Teatro Campesino, is that we achieve greater acceptance in Europe because in Europe they see us a little more clearly, ironi-cally enough. They see us as Mexicans or Chicanos or as Americans, but they *see* us. And they see what we do in a much clearer light. In this country, the descendants of all those European immigrants come to these shores cannot understand us. They cannot really see what we do. They cannot see the artistry of our work, or our art; they cannot see the veracity of our truths. Here we are ethnics, here we are a minority group. As a matter of fact, we are an extension of Mexico. But Mexico has yet to be recognized as the ancient capital of this part of the world. Who is fooling anybody? Mexico is the seat of civilization in this part of the world, with ancient cultural roots, but the only fact that is constantly recognized is that our people were "conquered." It was only until a few short years ago that Mexicanos were not outwardly identified as cowards and savages. The Sleepy Lagoon case involved some of this. Mexicans lost California and the Southwest because they were supposedly incapable of fighting to retain it. They were whipped and beaten by the United States. Consequently, they were cowards and every Mexican woman was a whore and that, in a broad sense, is still the underlying attitude toward Mexicans. At least that is still the image perpetrated in contemporary American literature, television and film.

Interviewer: One last statement from Paz. He says that Pachuco is "sheer negative impulse, a tangle of contradictions."

Valdez: That's assuming that contradiction is merely negative when actually contradiction is both good and bad, by its very nature, or it wouldn't be contradiction.

Interviewer: What about the "sheer negative impulse?"

Valdez: That's what I'm saying, a sheer negative impulse as opposed to what? What does he counterpose the Pachuco with, Octavio Paz? Octavio Paz is the positive? It's contradictory to say that the Pachuco's stance is sheer negative impulse, then to say in the same breath that he is full of contradictions. I'd say, who isn't? The nature of the human being is to be full of contradictions. The more contradictions you have under control the more sophisticated you are, but you've got to acknowledge the contradictions to begin with. I revel in the contradictions. I think that's what makes us human: our dichotomies. They make us interesting, so to contradict Octavio Paz: if the Pachuco is sheer negative impulse, he is also a sheer positive force.

Interviewer: I've heard people say he has retracted some of his statements. *Labyrinth* is still one of his most popular books. The academicians read it, the Anglo academicians, that is, and they believe what he said. They accept his interpretation at face value. This essay is a permanent document. And he hasn't, to my knowledge, revised the essay. This is why I'm interested in printing your interpretation of the Pachuco, so that we can better understand his life and his struggles.

Valdez: Well, I don't agree with some things I said ten years ago; so after thirty years, can you imagine. That's why I reserve the right to contradict myself. *Consafos*.

Victor Guerra

An Interview with Rodrigo Duarte of Teatro de la Esperanza

August 13, 1982/New York City

Víctor Guerra: Can you tell me briefly about the history of the group? How did it start?

Rodrigo Duarte: The group began at the University of California at Santa Barbara, as a student theater group, back in 1969. For two years it was called Teatro Mecha, because it was affiliated with MECHA. Then, after two years, it split from that organization and the name was changed to Teatro de la Esperanza. So Esperanza actually began in 1971. It stayed within the confines of the university for a couple more years, but it attached itself to a community center in Santa Barbara called La Casa de la Raza. Then it reached that point when the students graduate and they have to decide whether they're going to stay with the group or go on somewhere else. So it became for three or four years, a community-based theater, no longer a student group. It was a gradual transformation. And finally, from '76-77 it started transforming into a full-time theater company, which I guess is what we had envisioned becoming at some point. We started getting some grants, like CETA grants, to be able to dedicate ourselves more completely to the work, and we evolved into a full-time, "professional" theater company, and we continue to be that. There's a lot more to it, but that's the rough description.

Guerra: The play you performed the other night, *Hijos*, was written and directed collectively. How does that work?

Duarte: Well, you know, they had a discussion on this yesterday in one of the panels; some groups, when they talk about a collective creation, are talking about a process that starts after the text is written. In other words, they take a written piece and do improvs around it; the text is already written. But in our case we start from scratch. And in fact we start *before* the text. We start with what's going to be the theme and we have a discussion. Then we research and find out what it is we want to say about that particular theme.

And when that is semi-resolved, we more or less have a thesis with an argumentation to it. Then we start to put it into dramatic form.

Sometimes the two things are intertwined. For example, in our first play, we began investigating this one town, Guadalupe, which had all sorts of educational problems. We are basically just researching, but at the same time we started improvising around the research, taking pieces of information and trying to put them into dramatic form. As it turned out, we ended up doing a semi-documentary play; it was called *Guadalupe*. And so the research and the interviewing that we did with people ended up being also character studies, because some of the people that we were questioning became characters in the play. So the actor, at the same time that he was researching the theme, was also studying the characters, the characters that we would later be playing.

Anyway, the process of arriving at the text is a collective one, and we use different authors; a lot of people are involved in the actual scripting. But what's more important is that in the creation of the thesis and the argumentation and of the scenes by improvisation, all the actors are involved. So, in a sense, everybody has a creative force in the group.

The direction sometimes flows right out of this process, because we know what we want the play to say; we, the actors, know what we want to say. So the job of directing, then, becomes simpler, because everybody knows what we're striving for, and the director doesn't have to manipulate the actors to get them to do something.

But then, we do believe in expertise too. There are some people that are good writers, and so we put the writers to write. In order to arrive at a coherent piece, after everything's been written, sometimes we let one person go over it and give it a unified sense of dialogue and reshape certain things. We do have what we call a director, in the sense of a coordinator. He is the outside eye and he makes sure that the thing is saying what it's supposed to say. This last play was directed with three people—a committee of directors, with one clearly marked as the person that stops and starts—for organizational purposes. But at any given time, any one of the actors can talk to the three directors and say, "Listen, I don't think this scene is working, because of this and that." Of course, there are certain things that you've got to do. For instance, when we're rehearsing, it's hard for us to stop and have a long discussion, because the actors get cold. So it's not as chaotic as it might sound, because we've given it structure and organization. But it's still very much based on the fact that a lot of people have input, and that everybody has some capacity to direct or to see things in a scene that maybe somebody else has not seen. So, it's a complicated process that involves all kinds of discussion and development and thought. But we feel that it worked for us.

Guerra: Do you always work in that fashion? Do you ever take a play that's already an existing text?

Duarte: Since 1973 we have not done that. Although there is one case, where we took *La Orgía,* by Enrique Buenaventura, director-playwright for Teatro Experimental de Cali and had a person from outside the group come and direct it. And the process was clearly not collective. That was done for the purpose of training the actors and seeing another directorial method. We are not adverse to doing a play that's already written. In fact, if we would find something that we felt was apropos to what we were trying to do, we would definitely do that. It would relieve us of quite a bit of work. And we are not against a given actor writing a play; it doesn't have to be written collectively. I think we would envision in the future doing that. We have also thought about possibly adapting pieces. We have talked about adapting a Brecht play, for instance. I think we're all pretty open about our course in the future.

Guerra: How does being a collective manifest itself outside the plays?

Duarte: Well, I would like to differentiate between a collective and a commune. Not to use that last term negatively, but we're not in the "hippy" stage of the movement, where we all live in the same house and our kids are running around all over. But when we use the term collective, it does apply to various aspects of our work: in the art and in all the work of the group, which includes the administrative and technical.

   We approach it from the conviction that we have to change abruptly from the way of working that this capitalist society has. Our way of working is based on the ideological principle that we don't have a "patrón." That's the crux of it. But in our daily lives, we have sort of a family concept. Children's nurturing and raising belongs to the whole group. We're not a cult—we don't take the children away from the parents—but we do sense a responsibility as individual members of the group to raise the children. Everybody does child care. It's also a practical question. If you don't help the parents with their children, it's hard for them to work. But more than that, I think we see that the products of our labor belong to the whole. And so questions relating to how and what and so forth are determined by the collective. For example, we determine salary on the basis of need. Everybody gets a certain amount of money, and if you have a child you get more, because you have a greater need. If you have a specific problem that requires more salary for some reason, then it's determined on that basis.

Guerra: Where do you perform? Do you travel a lot?

Duarte: Yes, mostly we tour. We have a base, but we don't perform there as often. Santa Barbara's a difficult place to do any kind of an extended run. You exhaust your audience fairly quickly. So what we do is tour the Southwest, the Midwest. We have toured other places: Mexico, Europe, the East Coast a little bit. But the kind of place where we go to varies quite a bit—from prisons, community centers and labor camps to the other extreme: universities, performing arts centers and so forth. We try to do both.

We're essentially trying to reach the audiences that we have targeted: the working-class Chicano community is one, but also the general community, whether it be white or Chicano. We feel that what we have to say in the plays is good and valid for a lot of different people; we're not trying to limit our audience in any way. But there is a focus.

Guerra: And your themes are certainly *netamente chicano*.

Duarte: Right, they deal with the Chicano situation. All our collective works have dealt with some aspect of Chicano life. Now, there is a process that's occurring in the group, an ideological development, in a sense. You know, if you go back to the beginning of the Chicano Movement, there was a nationalist position, *mi raza primero*, but I think over the years we have become more flexible in our positions, and we see the Chicano as part of an international struggle, national and international. And we hook up with the Latin American situation. So we concentrate on the Chicano, but we are also trying to emphasize the fact that it's not an isolated movement, that our situation is akin to the situation in Brazil or Colombia or wherever. In fact, the last major play, *The Octopus*, deals with the worker in the United States, the Chicano in particular, and his relationship to international struggles. So, we have our focus, but it's broadening out.

Guerra: The Festival here called itself Festival de Teatro Popular. How do you define *teatro popular* in relation to yourselves?

Duarte: It's a tricky, almost semantic, question that's developed. Yesterday, for example, Enrique Buenaventura denounced populism in terms of the theater. And he had his specific reasons, right? So when you say popular theater, you almost have to define what you mean by it. Essentially, there's a question of what does "popular" mean. For example, punk rock might be popular or disco music might be popular. Ronnie Davis of the San Francisco Mime Troupe pointed out that in Nicaragua when he went there, there were 200 revolutionaries dancing to disco music. So disco music had become part of the Sandinista revolution. He was trying to show that what the people like, what's popular, isn't necessarily positive, that being popular isn't the single most important thing, that you will have to select.

With us it's a practical question. What we, Teatro de la Esperanza, mean by *popular* is the kind of theater that is built to communicate with the majority of people, which are working-class people and, in our case, they are Chicanos. So we're not talking about levels. A lot of people when they say "popular theater" say, "You have to go down to their level"; it's very paternalistic, condescending. And we're not talking about popular theater meaning that you almost have to simplify everything so that they can understand it. The question is not one of making the plays less sophisticated or complex; it's a question of dealing with the play in a way that's understandable, using symbols that are common to those people. For example, if you were to do a Chicano play using Shakespearean terminology, they don't know that language. It's not that they're any less intelligent; it's just that culturally that's not part of their reality, that's not part of their life. When I first read Shakespeare I couldn't understand it. And it didn't mean that I was stupid; I just didn't know that kind of language. So you take a play by Ibsen that uses certain symbols, or Greek plays; if you don't know the gods, the Greek pantheon, then it doesn't make sense what the chorus might say. So all that stuff has to be something that's common to them. Common, and that emerges or surges from that particular cultural context. And that's all we're saying: make the plays such that the symbols are common to them and don't bring in foreign symbols that might be misunderstood, that might endanger the possibility of your communication with the audience. But no, don't make it any less sophisticated, don't make it any less complex. Our audiences are perhaps not educated in the formal sense, but they're definitely intelligent. There's no having to defend that.

I think that's what Buenaventura was talking about when he was attacking populism, that people are saying, "Make it so simple that a first-grader can understand it."

Guerra: Who are the members of Teatro la Esperanza? Can you tell me something about them?

Duarte: Well, we have nine people in the group; I'll start from the oldest, in terms of experience.

José Saucedo has had the most years in the group. He started in 1970-71, and with a one-and-a-half year interruption when he went to Colombia—where he worked with Teatro Experimental de Cali—and Venezuela, he's been in the group consistently during that time. He's probably the best director in the group, a key person within the group. He's a theater major out of UC Santa Barbara.

The next one would be me, Rodrigo Duarte Clark. I was a political science major and active in the student movement at that time, and I participated with the Teatro sort of indirectly at first. Later on, when I graduated and I was teaching high school, I became involved as a writer; I'd taken a class and written a couple of things and the group put them on. Later on they asked me to participate as a writer and little by little incorporated me as an actor, and pretty soon I was involved in just about everything. So I've been with the group since '73. My main thing is writing. I would at some point like to write something on my own; it's a different process, but I look forward to that. I might get to take a leave of absence soon.

The next person in terms of length of time in the group is José Luis Valenzuela, who played the father of *Hijos*. He's a *mexicano;* he came to the United States and joined a group in the Bay Area called Teatro de la Gente, and he stayed with them for two years and, obviously talented, he became one of the main actors in the group. But he left that group for his own reasons and joined our group in 1978. He's very sharp ideologically; he's been a major influence.

The next one is Rubén Castro, another *mexicano* who came to the U.S. with a performing group from Mexico and stayed. It's a long story. But, he joined the group at the end of '78. He found a friend in Santa Barbara and he married, and his *compañera*, in effect, is part of the group. She's not a member of the group—she doesn't act—but she necessarily is a part of the family. He's an important actor.

The next would be—I'll bring them in as a family—Rupert and Joann Reyes and their two children. They joined at the end of '78. Rupert joined and then she came with him and decided she wanted to do the same thing, although she was more into the administrative side and he was more into the artistic. They stayed with the group for a period of time but then left and moved back to Texas, because they were separated from their blood family; they left after they had their first child. But they found that they wanted to come back, that they missed the work and that they liked the family concept. Even though they did have their own family, they also wanted to be part of this family. So they came back and they've been in the group since, and now they have another child.

Rupert is a graduate of the drama department at the University of Texas at Austin. Joann also went to UT but her emphasis was teaching; she has her credentials and was a teacher for some time. In the group she acts as the tour coordinator. She also has a lot of input into the development of the family concept and child raising.

She's very well-read on that subject. She has a lot to offer to the group.

Ana would be the next person. Ana Olivares has been with the group about three years beginning in 1980. Hers is an interesting case. She belonged to a group in Texas that had fallen apart, like I guess most of the groups had. Yet she, as an actress, was not very developed; in fact, she was weak. But her commitment to doing theater was strong, and her political base was strong. Her potential, attracted us enough to her to give her an audition and then to accept her into the group. And over the years it's been a real rewarding experience for all of us, because now she's a very talented actress. She still has room to develop, but from where she came to where she is has been a giant step. She's also a poet and she's helped in some of the writing.

The next person is Evelina Fernández; she came in 1981. She's almost the newest to the group, but she's been in Chicano theater since 1975. She was also in the original cast of Zoot Suit. So she was in Chicano theater before what could be considered, you know, "theater at the Mark Taper Forum" . . . She's very intelligent, very politically developed and she's got a whole lot of talent. And as an actress she's developed a great deal in the group. She's tried out a whole lot of different roles that were very challenging, so it's allowed her to grow. But we've discovered that she's also a writer and she also has directorial capacity and she's a dancer.

Then the last person is Raquel Salinas, who joined us just a month ago. She's an ex-member of Teatro Primavera and has been around theater in the Los Angeles area. She joined right before this trip to New York. And I'm sure it's been difficult for her having to incorporate herself as an actress into a group of people that she really didn't know a whole lot, and leaving her home. But it's also very exciting, I think.

Now the kids: we have Fidel, Evelina's little boy, and José Luis's; and Rupert and Joann have Julio. And they just had a little girl named Carina, who was born while we were on tour. Then we have my little girl, Marisol, who's four years old. She lives in San José and she comes every two months for approximately three weeks, and the group takes care of her when she's here. So the kids range from four years old to Carina, who's four months old.

Guerra: What other Chicano teatros are functioning, at a national level?

Duarte: Well, there are no other groups that are actually touring. Teatro Campesino immediately comes to mind, of course, but they have changed their whole way of operating. They are now more or less a production company and they don't tour as much. Most of their shows are presented in San Juan Bautista, California where they are based, and they audition actors, do a set production and then the actors leave.

Now and then they will tour; they'll tour a specific production to Europe or something like that, but it's only in specific situations. It's hard to understand everything about how they are operating. But there are no full-time *teatros* except for Teatro Campesino and ourselves.

Apart from these two there are a lot of small groups in California that are still doing *teatro* and sometimes touring. And I can mention some of them. There's Teatro Gusto and Teatro Latino in the Bay Area. And there's a women's group that developed last year, Valentina Productions it's called, in San José; they do women's plays. Teatro Urbano, which is an old group, still fucntions in Los Angeles. Primavera and Teatro Mestizo are functioning from time to time, but not fully. There's a new group that started about a year ago, but that has some old people, Teatro Café, from Los Angeles, based at the Inner City Cultural Center. It's a lot of young people with a few older ones that have some experience. Outside of California there's Teatro Libertad in Tucson; there's a couple of *teatros* in the Midwest that we know of; there's Teatro Bilingüe in Houston; there are groups in Denver: Su Teatro and Teatro de la Causa.

Now apart from those groups, the Chicano groups that have that trajectory of political theater, there are other groups that have developed more mainstream. For example, in Los Angeles there's the Bilingual Arts Foundation with Carmen Zapata as director. They are kind of a production company, and they do cultural things, things that are Latino; sometimes they'll take a traditional play and Latinize it. It's similar to Miriam Colón's Puerto Rican Traveling Theatre in New York. It has a different ideological basis and a different purpose. They are Latinos and they do Latino theater, but it means something slightly different. It's committed to change within theater, that Latinos are going to do these kinds of plays, but it's a different trajectory; it's not committed to a social change. But, you know, they are a Chicano theater too; we might disagree with their purposes, but when we're talking about Chicano theater they are definitely a force, and they definitely have to be talked to and related to and perhaps we can find a way of helping both.

Guerra: What plans do you have for the future?

Duarte: We have in mind what we call an "institute of Chicano theater" that we're trying to establish in Santa Barbara. It's a long-term project which requires that we start working now. What we want to start with is a six-week, prolonged *seminario* on Chicano theater, with perhaps a couple of plays being mounted and staged. It's been kind of a project of TENAZ, Teatros Nacionales de Aztlan, the organization of Chicano theaters in the Southwest. What we're trying to do is give the active Chicano participants in theater a chance to train, to develop their skills, to develop theoretically. So that the kind of theater that is being done advances. We also wish to bring in international support to it, meaning people outside of Chicano theater, both in the United States and outside the United States. For instance, we hope to have a Cuban director come in and perhaps direct and display his directorial methodology. Also possibly Santiago García from Colombia. And not only in terms of directing, but perhaps also acting teachers, writing coaches, administrators, the entire gamut of the theatre. And, of course, our problems are going to be logistical and financial. So we're focusing at first on something a bit more limited: six weeks. And we hope that eventually we would have a school of theater that people could come to and receive some concrete help in terms of developing. But again, the emphasis is on the active participant in theater, not the Chicano who aspires to Hollywood, but the people within the Chicano theater movement that have a progressive bent, that are going to do popular theater.